Contents

Furth
Raisi
Life C

Presented to Parliament by
the Secretary of State for Education and Skills
by Command of Her Majesty

March 2006

Cm 6768

£17.50

Foreword

Our economic future depends on our productivity as a nation. That requires a labour force with skills to match the best in the world.

This is a huge challenge, because there are some deep-seated and long-standing weaknesses in our national skills. We have put in place major reform programmes for 14-19 year olds and adult skills, backed by substantial investment. Those reforms are bringing about real progress. But there is a long way to go to raise skills and qualification levels for young people and adults to world standards.

We must set a new ambition to tackle once and for all those skills weaknesses. The colleges and training providers that make up the Further Education sector are central to achieving that ambition. There is much to be proud of in our Further Education system, with some excellent colleges. But at present, Further Education is not achieving its full potential as the powerhouse of a high skills economy.

This White Paper sets out the reforms needed to realise that potential. They build on the public sector reform principles we have applied in other services, including more choice for customers, tailoring services to meet individuals' needs, encouraging new, innovative providers to enter the market, and robust action to tackle poor quality combined with more autonomy for the excellent.

Our reforms will renew the mission of the Further Education system, and its central role in equipping young people and adults with the skills for productive, sustainable employment in a modern economy. They will provide new incentives for colleges to develop distinctive areas of specialist excellence. They will put the needs and interests of learners and employers at the heart of the system, so that their choices drive funding and performance management. They will create a new entitlement, backed by additional funding announced in the Budget, to free training and support for those young people who most need it, to get the qualifications for good, high-skill jobs.

We will develop a new national strategy for raising the quality of teaching and learning in Further Education, with robust intervention to tackle failing and mediocre provision, combined with more autonomy for the excellent. We will invest more in recruiting and training the best staff, with a stronger flow of business expertise coming into the sector and more college staff helped to gain workplace experience. Through federations and trusts we will encourage innovation. Through competitions we will enable new providers to enter the market. Funding systems will be reformed to reward those who respond to customer demand. There will be greater clarity of roles and responsibilities at every level, with more freedom of manoeuvre for good colleges and training providers and streamlined administration.

Through these reforms we will enable the Further Education sector to rise to the challenge. Evolutionary and incremental change will not be enough. We need fundamental reform in the role colleges and training providers play. Thereby they will achieve their rightful place in public esteem, valued by the public as essential pathways to good jobs and rewarding lives, and respected by employers as key partners in building successful businesses.

Tony Blair
Prime Minister

Ruth Kelly
Secretary of State for Education and Skills

Gordon Brown
Chancellor of the Exchequer

Executive summary

Purpose

1. Our future as a prosperous nation depends on our education and training system. We rely on that system to prepare young people fully for life, and to develop in both young people and adults the skills that are necessary for the productive and competitive economy that underpins our quality of life and many of our wider national ambitions.

2. We need to support people to develop skills in the broadest sense: enabling and equipping them to deploy to best effect their talent, knowledge, resourcefulness and creativity. That is the core purpose of the colleges and training providers that make up our Further Education (FE) system. The system serves many 16-19 year-olds – studying general and vocational qualifications, Apprenticeships and other forms of work based training. Some 4.6 million adults over the age of 19 study in FE every year, on a huge range of courses from basic skills through to Foundation Degrees.

3. The FE system must be the powerhouse for delivering the skills at all levels that are needed to sustain an advanced, competitive economy and make us a fairer society, offering equal opportunities for all based on talent and effort, not background.

The challenge of skills

4. There is much to celebrate in our FE system. We have some excellent colleges and training providers. The system has demonstrated great flexibility in adapting to new

challenges, is effective in reflecting and responding to the diversity of local communities, and has a strong track record in tackling inequality and reducing achievement gaps.

5. Recent improvements in results achieved by the education and training system owe a great deal to FE: the significant increase in the proportion of 19 year-olds achieving Level 2 qualifications – up 3 percentage points to 69.8%; the improvement in completion rates for full Apprenticeship frameworks from 31% in 2003/04 to 40% in 2004/05; the recent increase in post-16 participation to new record levels; and the overall improvement in success rates in FE from 59% in 2000/01 to 72% in 2003/04.

6. Those achievements are a tribute to the skill, dedication and hard work of all those working in the FE system. They have been supported by substantial investment. Since 1997, participation in post-16 training has expanded, with total learner numbers rising from around 4 million in 1997/98 to around 6 million in 2004/05. The Government has increased investment in colleges by 48% in real terms between 1997/98 and 2005/06. Through the formation of the Learning and Skills Council (LSC), we have brought together for the first time all forms of funding for post-16 education, training and skills outside Higher Education (HE), so that we can tackle the artificial funding and organisational barriers between different parts of the system.

7. Yet, despite this progress, by international standards, we face major areas of weakness. The proportion of our young people staying on in education and training post-16 is scandalously low: the UK ranks 24th out of 29 developed nations. We lag well behind France and Germany in the proportion of our young adults achieving a Level 3 qualification in their early twenties. The number of adults in the workforce without the skills at Level 2 for productive, sustainable employment in a modern economy is much too high: in that area we rank 17th out of 30 countries. All this makes clear that as a nation we need to raise our ambitions for skills.

8. Through the 14-19 and skills strategies we have already put in place far-reaching reforms to address these weaknesses. But we have to speed up progress. The initial report in autumn 2005 by Lord Leitch on the skills needs of the economy in 2020 presents a daunting picture of the rate at which other nations such as China and India are improving their skills base, and the challenge we must set ourselves if we are to keep pace. Even achieving all our current targets for raising skills among young people and adults would mean that in 2020 we would be no better than mediocre in the international rankings.

9. None of us should be willing to settle for that as the limit of our aspiration. Our aim must be to be leading the world in skills development – with virtually all young people staying on to age 19 and half going on to HE; all adults having the support

they need to up-skill and re-skill throughout life; all employers seeing skills as key to their success. From this can come productivity growth that will sustain us as a leading world economy.

Reform principles

10. We will only achieve this if our FE system is fit for purpose in meeting the two strategic challenges of transforming 14-19 education and up-skilling the adult workforce. This will mean major reform for colleges and training providers, so that FE gains the esteem it deserves as the engine room of a successful economy, with the power to transform lives.

11. The reform agenda since 1997 has provided us with evidence and key lessons that we will build on. We know that offering high quality vocational learning to 14-16 year olds, often in colleges, can help boost post-16 staying on rates; and that delivering well-designed training at work can result in employees getting a higher rate of return from the qualifications they gain. We know that encouraging colleges to work with employers and specialise in particular occupational areas can raise performance; and that giving employers and learners greater choice in the design and delivery of training raises their motivation and satisfaction.

12. The measures set out in this White Paper build on these lessons and on the public service reform principles that the Government has adopted in other sectors, most recently in the *Higher Standards, Better Schools for All* White Paper on school reform. We are raising the bar on standards, with a tough approach to both inadequate and coasting providers; encouraging a diverse and high quality set of providers; promoting learner choice; tailoring provision so that is responsive to the needs of all learners; and ensuring there is clarity of role between commissioners, providers and regulators, with a reduction in bureaucracy across the whole system.

13. This White Paper builds on recent secondary school reforms, the 14-19 and skills strategies, the Success for All programme, and the LSC's *agenda for change* reforms. It also responds to the important independent report published recently by Sir Andrew Foster on the future role of colleges. It sets out a far-reaching programme of reform in six main areas.

Mission and specialisation

14. As the Foster report said, this challenge means that we need to establish a clear mission for FE, focused on the employability and progression of learners. This is central to delivering the skills and qualifications which individuals, employers and the economy need.

15. So we will put the economic mission of the sector at the heart of its role. That means defining its central purpose as being to equip young people and adults with the skills, competences and qualifications that employers want, and which will prepare them for productive, rewarding, high-value employment in a modern economy. This includes developing the skills and attributes for enterprise and self-employment.

16. The delivery of this new mission will involve the creation of a new specialist system. We will expect every FE provider to develop one or more areas of specialist excellence, which will become central to the mission and ethos of the institution and will drive its improvement. A new, more powerful phase of the successful programme of Centres of Vocational Excellence (CoVEs) will be central to this. This will include a new, higher standard for accreditation, a more direct role for employers and stronger encouragement to develop several CoVEs in related disciplines within a single institution. We will extend the programme of National Skills Academies (NSAs) as part of this drive for specialisation.

17. As well as encouraging a much clearer focus within colleges, we will form strong specialist networks between colleges in every major economic sector. New, national sector-based networks of vocational providers led by NSAs will be increasingly important in driving improvement. These networks will be characterised by their strong links with employers, raising standards, reputation and motivation.

18. We will promote a stronger and growing Sixth Form College sector. The FE system as a whole has a crucial role in delivering 14-19 reform, but Sixth Form Colleges' role is particularly central. Sixth Form Colleges will increasingly broaden the curriculum and qualifications they offer as part of 14-19 reform, and will offer some courses to 14-16 year-olds. We will recognise particularly effective provision in Sixth Form Colleges through a new 'Centre of Excellence' designation.

19. This economic mission does not mean narrow vocationalism. It includes for instance the general education that employers value and the stepping stone provision that helps prepare people for success in life and work as well as provision at Levels 2 and 3. We will strengthen the role of colleges and training providers in providing HE programmes linked to their economic and social mission. We will develop colleges' role in HE in regions where access to HE institutions is limited, through the lifelong learning network programme. There are ten such networks in operation, with more in development. We will target new networks where currently provision is most sparse. We will explore, with the Higher Education Funding Council for England and the LSC, how we might offer better capital support to enable FE providers to contribute to HE. We will prioritise the development of some larger college providers of HE as centres of excellence, with a major part to play in developing work based HE programmes for employers.

20. The economic mission will not be the sector's sole purpose. Education and training for personal fulfilment, community development and the love of learning all have an important place and will be sustained, though the pattern of institutions specialising in such programmes is likely to change. As general FE colleges increasingly focus on the core economic mission, local authority and voluntary providers may focus on wider personal fulfilment and community programmes, with funding targeted on securing high quality provision which meets local community priorities.

Meeting employer and learner needs

21. Alongside this stronger sense of purpose, we want to make a decisive shift towards a system that is driven by the needs of service users. We will introduce measures that put learners and employers in the driving seat in determining what is funded and how services are delivered.

22. A programme of learner accounts will be trialled, focused on helping people gain Level 3 qualifications. We know that accounts can have a powerful effect in motivating learners, creating a sense of ownership, and attracting them back into learning. We will also make sure that all colleges have learner representatives on their governing body.

23. We also need to do more to help those of today's young adults who do not achieve a Level 3 qualification by the age of 19. Under the current system there is a sharp cliff edge in support post-19, for instance in relation to tuition fees. Yet for many young people, particularly from disadvantaged backgrounds, their early twenties is the time when they wish to gain Level 3 qualifications to give them a step up to a better job. So we will create a new entitlement to free training to enable young people to complete their initial education and training to Level 3 up to the age of 25. Through the continuing roll out of the Adult Learning Grant (ALG), we will also provide help with maintenance costs for those on low incomes.

24. For employers, who too often feel that colleges and training providers are not responsive enough to their needs, we will roll out the pioneering Train to Gain programme. This helps employers, supported by brokers, get training delivered in the workplace to meet their needs. It offers full public funding for basic employability skills and we have already committed to trials that will extend this to cover qualifications at Level 3. We will now extend it further to test the introduction of work based training at HE level as well. This means that for the first time, an employer will be able to source all their skills needs – from adult basic literacy to degree level engineering – through a single broker.

25. These changes will be underpinned by qualification reform which ensures better progression routes for young people (through specialised Diplomas) and greater simplicity and navigability for adults (through the Framework for Achievement).

A national strategy for better teaching and learning

26. We need a world class education and training system that provides a high quality learning experience for all, making effective use of new technology. Given the investment of time, and in many cases their own money, that students are making we must ensure that quality is right every time. Colleges and providers will be responsible for driving up quality within their own organisations, with an increasing emphasis on self-improvement.

27. For the first time, a single Quality Improvement Agency will be responsible for supporting providers in this role. It will lead the implementation of a single, national Quality Improvement Strategy for teaching and learning in FE. There will be new support for teaching staff in FE, including through the development of new teaching and learning materials, backed by subject coaches, especially to support delivery of the specialised Diplomas. The Strategy will support increasing personalisation, so that individual needs and circumstances are built into the design and delivery of education and training.

28. The Strategy will be backed by new measures to support the development of the workforce. Staff need to be properly trained and to develop and update their skills regularly to respond to changing needs and new challenges. We will introduce a Continuing Professional Development (CPD) requirement, so that all staff are required to undertake a minimum amount of CPD each year. New programmes will be introduced to boost recruitment of talented graduates; encourage highly effective managers from other sectors to come in to FE; provide opportunities for skilled specialists to teach in FE; and provide opportunities for FE staff to update their skills in industry. All new college principals will need to gain a new leadership qualification. Building on the good work of the Network of Black Managers and the Centre for Excellence in Leadership in relation to race equality, the quality strategy will be centred on a powerful commitment to equality and diversity.

Spreading success and eliminating failure

29. We will support the development of the more personalised system we seek, by taking decisive action to eliminate failure and creating structures that help the best providers to spread their influence.

30. There is now much less failing and unsatisfactory provision in FE than in the recent past. We are now raising the bar to ensure that all provision is good or improving.

Any provider or provision judged to be failing or coasting will be subject to an improvement notice. Colleges and other providers will receive support to address the problems immediately. If the problems are not addressed within a year, the LSC will be able to act decisively – changing governors, changing the leadership of the college, opening up the provision to competition or seeking merger with or help from a strong provider.

31. At the same time, we will encourage new structural models, including federations, collaborative partnerships and Trusts to make it easier for the best providers to spread their influence across the system and lead change. In addition, there will be a presumption that colleges meeting criteria to be designated 'high performing' will be able to expand their provision for 14-19 year olds, particularly to provide new Diplomas.

32. To promote dynamism and innovation we will encourage new high quality providers into the FE sector. New competition arrangements will make it easier for new providers to enter the system, where significant expansion of high quality provision is needed. There will be open advertising, with appropriate development funding and capital incentives, as well as revenue funding, for the successful provider. This will enable good existing colleges to expand, federate or create a Trust, independent and voluntary sector training providers to enter the sector, or wholly new institutions to be established, depending on needs. It will be underpinned by a new LSC remit to promote diversity, choice and specialisation.

33. A new balanced scorecard and single performance indicator (along the lines of the local authority CPA system) will support college self-improvement, provide greater transparency and information for learners, and strengthen public accountability for colleges.

Funding

34. We need a funding system which supports the FE system to move in the direction outlined here. Funding will be targeted on priority areas and follow the needs of learners and employers. For 14-19, that means a new approach which provides fair funding for comparable activity across all institutions; and support for young people to make the best choices for them, including choosing to study and train for part of their programme at another institution. We have already significantly reduced the funding gap between schools and colleges, and will continue to close the gap as resources allow. For adults, we will progressively build up the proportion of funding that is demand-led and driven by customer choice – particularly through the Train to Gain programme and trials of learner accounts. By 2010, our ambition is that some

40% of the total adult skills budget could be allocated through these demand-led routes, with the majority demand-led by 2015.

35. The new entitlement to free tuition for all 19-25 year-olds studying for their first Level 3 qualification will be funded in full, while for other provision we will move towards a 50% fee contribution for adults who are not entitled to free tuition. We will continue to support low-income learners to ensure that they are not prevented from participating in priority programmes and will extend the ALG to full national coverage from September 2007, to help meet the additional costs of learning.

36. These proposals will be backed by regional and local plans to improve the quality and diversity of provision, determining the pattern of new capital investment. Local authorities will be asked to expand the scope of Building Schools for the Future visions to include FE provision for 14-19 year-olds, so that they are fully comprehensive in setting out what will be required in a locality to deliver our 14-19 reform programme. LSC capital will be directed to implementing this vision, alongside BSF resources. Additionally, we do not want differences in the way capital projects are funded in schools and colleges to get in the way of each local area making the right decisions about the best pattern of institutions to meet 14-19 needs, so we will look to create a more level playing field for capital funding, while continuing to take account of the scope to draw on other sources of income.

A new relationship with colleges and providers

37. A central finding of the Foster report was that the FE system is over-regulated and too complex. We agree. If colleges and training providers are to meet the challenge we are setting, they must have the space and freedom to do so.

38. We will implement a simplified system for planning and funding provision, which will make clearer the links between national priorities and local action, and enable colleges to play more fully to their strengths. A single named strategic partner will lead for the LSC in its relationship with each college or provider. There will be improved communications between Government and its agencies and the FE system: there will be a single gateway process for all publications and data returns, which will ensure that only relevant, clear and important communications are sent as a matter of course to providers. Improved arrangements for data collection will ensure that data is collected once and used many times. There will be new freedoms from the planning infrastructure for the most effective providers.

39. There will be clarity of roles and less bureaucracy at every level. The DfES will in the future focus on its core purpose of strategic leadership and policy formulation. By withdrawing from operational activity and making savings, it will reduce its staff working on the learning and skills sector by some 325 between 2004 and 2008.

The LSC will remain the key body responsible for planning and funding the FE system, ensuring the right pattern of colleges and providers are delivering high quality programmes. The LSC has already committed to reduce staffing by 1,100 by the end of 2007. To ensure that the FE system is fit for purpose to meet the 14-19 and adults skills challenges, the LSC will need to continue to reform in line with the direction of travel that it set out in *agenda for change*.

40. To play the role set out in this White Paper, the LSC will strengthen its regional capacity. This is necessary to oversee the performance of general FE colleges, to plan with regional partners the skills infrastructure needed across the area to meet the needs of employers and adults, and to oversee competitions for new provision.

41. We are legislating to provide a new curriculum and qualifications entitlement for 14-19 year-olds, through the current Education and Inspection Bill. This will place new duties to secure sufficient provision to meet the entitlement, on local authorities in relation to 14-16 year-olds, and on the LSC for 16-19 year-olds. Both the local authority and LSC have crucial roles in delivery and their funding powers will need to be used to enable them to play those roles effectively. We want local authorities to play the strategic leadership role, consistent with their leadership role in children's services overall, ensuring the integration of the delivery of 14-19 reform with the wider agenda for children and young people in the locality. Within that, the LSC remains the primary partner for the local authority, using its funding and powers to secure rapid and high quality implementation of the 16-19 entitlement in every area. In practice, we want to see local authorities and the LSC working together to drive progress through a shared strategy, as many are already doing. We will work through Government Offices and the LSC to ensure that there are arrangements in place in each area to monitor delivery of 14-19 reform and the new statutory entitlements in particular, and to intervene if necessary.

42. In the major cities, including London, we want much stronger links between jobs, adult training, regeneration and economic development, all with a strong employer lead. So we will be working with major cities to form new partnerships involving the LSC, the city council, Jobcentre Plus, the Regional Development Agency, and employers. The LSC will work with local authorities more broadly to ensure that the skills agenda is reflected in Local Area Agreements as they are extended to all parts of the country.

43. The more powerful regional role, together with the local partnership teams and stronger links between jobs, training and skills in cities, means that the current structure of 47 local LSCs will need to change. We will ask the Chair of the LSC to advise on a new, streamlined accountability structure, which secures strong engagement of employers and other stakeholders.

44. These reforms are all part of the LSC strengthening its capacity to work strategically with colleges and providers, while withdrawing from much day to day administrative activity. Further simplification and reduction of bureaucracy will come through reform of the inspection, quality improvement, qualifications and data collection operations. The overall effect will be to create a better balance of autonomy and accountability for colleges, with more discretion for good providers to decide how to respond to customer needs, combined with sharper LSC intervention to sort out poor and mediocre provision.

Impact

45. By 2008 the measures set out in this White Paper will have led to real benefits for learners and employers. Amongst these:

- young people will be benefiting from five new specialised Diplomas, with all 14 Diplomas available nationwide by 2013;
- adults will be benefiting from the first stages of a clearer, simpler, qualifications framework, designed by employers and fully implemented from 2010;
- 19-25 year-olds will be benefiting from a new entitlement to free tuition for their first full Level 3 qualification, which will be extended over time as the new qualification framework is introduced, to cover the lower level courses that provide the best stepping stones through to Level 3;
- adults in pilot regions will be benefiting from a learning account giving them funds towards the cost of a Level 3 course at a provider of their choice, together with information and advice tailored to their needs;
- employers throughout the country will be benefiting from training delivered in the workplace, by a provider of their choosing, delivered to suit their operational needs. Training for basic skills and Level 2 will be free, and there will be access to Level 3 and HE.

46. In addition by 2008 there will be a new dynamism within the system:

- All FE colleges will have a clear economic mission, specialising in areas of distinctive excellence. Standards will be improved by strong specialist networks across colleges and training providers.
- New high quality providers will be encouraged to enter the FE sytem to drive up standards, raise innovation, and expand the range of training available. The LSC will have stopped funding any inadequate colleges, providers or departments, levering up standards through radical change such as merger or federation with another stronger college, or a change in leadership.

- There will be much closer collaboration between schools and colleges, with 14-19 pupils able to study courses in the institution best placed to meet their needs and interests. There will be a closer relationship between colleges and universities, with easy progression from Level 3 onto Foundation Degrees, and from there onto honours degree courses.

47. Through these changes, the FE system will realise its potential to be a key driver of economic growth and competitiveness and an engine of social justice and equality of opportunity.

Chapter 1: Introduction

1.1 There is much to celebrate in our Further Education (FE) system. We have some excellent colleges and training providers. Success rates are rising fast. More young people and adults gain good qualifications every year. We now have a strong Apprenticeships programme. Over a million people have been helped to improve their basic literacy, numeracy and language skills. The system has demonstrated great flexibility in adapting to new challenges and meeting new targets. It is effective in reflecting and responding to the diversity of local communities and has a strong track record in tackling inequality and reducing achievement gaps.

1.2 Recent improvements in results achieved by the education and training system owe a great deal to FE: the significant increase in the proportion of 19 year-olds achieving Level 2 qualifications – up 3 percentage points to 69.8%; the improvement in completion rates for full Apprenticeship frameworks from 31% in 2003/4 to 40% in 2004/5; the recent increase in post-16 participation to new record levels; and the overall improvement in success rates in FE from 59% in 2000/01 to 72% in 2003/04.

1.3 Those improvements are a tribute to the skill, dedication and hard work of all those working in the FE system. They have been supported by substantial investment. Since 1997, participation in post-16 training has expanded, with total learner numbers rising from around 4 million in 1997/98 to around 6 million in 2004/05. We have increased investment in colleges by 48% in real terms between 1997/98 and 2005/06. Through the formation of the Learning and Skills Council (LSC), we have brought together for the first time all forms of funding for post-16 education, training and skills outside Higher Education (HE), so that we can tackle the artificial funding and organisational barriers between different parts of the sector.

1.4 Yet, despite this progress, by international standards, we face major areas of weakness. The proportion of our young people staying on in education and training post-16 is scandalously low: the UK ranks 24th out of 29 developed nations. We lag well behind France and Germany in the proportion of our young adults achieving a Level 3 qualification in their early twenties. The number of adults in the workforce without the skills for productive, sustainable employment in a modern economy is much too high: in that area we rank 17th out of 30 countries. All this makes clear that as a nation we need to raise our ambitions for skills. Given demographic changes, it will not be enough simply to improve the skills of young people entering the labour market: there must be major improvements in the skills of adults too.

1.5 And there are still significant issues to address in the FE system: 2% of colleges are currently assessed by inspectors as inadequate, 20% of colleges have at least one curriculum area regarded as unsatisfactory, and 5% of leadership and management in colleges is unsatisfactory. Inspection results for work-based learning during the past year indicated that 12% of providers were inadequate, 13% of work-based areas of learning were unsatisfactory, and 11% of leadership and management was unsatisfactory. Welfare recipients need better support to gain skills for sustainable employment, particularly as a route out of benefit dependency. We are not doing enough to engage employers or address their needs. 7% of employers who used FE colleges during the last year were 'not very' or 'not at all' satisfied with provision. 82% of employers did not use colleges at all[1]. More work needs to be done to close the gap in success rates between minority ethnic groups and white learners, and to tackle the historically low entry rates of women and minority ethnic groups into work-based training.

1.6 In coming to the next stage of reform, we have learnt from the changes already put in place and will build on that experience. The successes of Skills for Life and Success for All provide the strong base from which to build. We know that offering high quality vocational learning to 14-16 year olds, often in colleges, can help increase participation post-16. Delivering high quality training in the workplace helps employees get a higher rate of return from the qualifications they gain. Encouraging colleges to engage with employers and specialise in particular areas can raise their performance.

1 National Employers Skills Survey 2005

1.7 In the last year, we have set out on the basis of this experience two major reform strategies which will demand significant changes to the FE system. Each is driven by the needs of learners, society and the wider economy:

- Our strategy for reform of education and training for 14-19 year-olds. Through this, we aim to transform opportunity and achievement for young people, so that all young people are prepared by their education to succeed in life – and so that we move from 75% participation at age 17 to 90% participation. The FE system has a major role to play in delivering this strategy – including through offering more opportunities to 14-16 year-olds and implementing the new Diploma qualifications.
- Our adult skills strategy. Through this, we are seeking to create a step change in the level of skills in the workforce. Building on the success of Skills for Life in driving up basic skills, we are seeking sharply to cut the number of adults without at least the Level 2 skills which are the threshold for employment. The strategy sets out a major shift towards a system shaped by the demands of learners and employers.

1.8 These strategies put in place some stretching targets. We are committed to increasing participation among 16-19 year-olds from 75% now to 90% in 2015. In 2005, 69.8% of young people had achieved a Level 2 qualification by age 19, an increase of 3 percentage points in a year. We expect to see further year on year increases, as well as continued increases in Level 3 attainment. We want to increase the number of young people successfully completing an Apprenticeship by 75% by 2007/08. By 2010, we want 2.25 million adults to improve their literacy and numeracy skills, and some 3.6 million adults to gain the platform of employability skills represented by a full Level 2 qualification. And we continue to work towards 50% of 18 to 30 year olds participating in Higher Education (HE).

1.9 These two key strategies and associated targets place major demands on the FE system. At the same time, the targets for international excellence that we seek to achieve are themselves rising fast. The interim report, published in December 2005, by Lord Leitch[2] on the skills needs of the economy in 2020 presents a daunting picture of the rate at which other nations such as China and India are improving their skills base, and the challenge we must set ourselves if we are to keep pace. Even achieving all our current targets for raising skills among young people and adults, would still leave us no better than mediocre in the international rankings in 2020.

1.10 None of us should be willing to settle for that as the limit of our aspiration. We want virtually all our young people to stay on in post-compulsory education and training to gain good skills and qualifications and half to go on to HE to gain the advanced

2 Lord Leitch, *Skills in the UK: The long-term challenge, Interim report* (December 2005)

qualifications the economy increasingly demands. We want all adults to have support and encouragement to up-skill and re-skill throughout their working lives, with free entitlements for all to get the platform of skills for productive, sustainable employment. We want all employers to see training and skills as essential investments for business success.

1.11 These twin, urgent requirements – a transformation of the life chances of young people and of the skills of the workforce – are the drivers for the reforms set out in this White Paper. If the challenges are to be met in full, then FE must play a central role in meeting them. In order for it do so, a significant programme of change is required.

1.12 This is the case set out powerfully in Sir Andrew Foster's recent report on the future of FE colleges, *Realising the Potential*, to which this White Paper is a response. As that report argued, the system must focus ever more closely on its role in the transformation of life chances implied by 14-19 reform and the task of meeting the challenge set by the global economy and articulated in the Leitch review. This focus implies a clearer mission for FE than it has had before – centred on developing the skills and attributes required for employment and meeting the demands of the economy. It also implies a reconfiguration of the system around this mission. The public response to the Foster report, and the consultations that have informed this White Paper, have indicated a widespread recognition of the need for reform.

1.13 Our vision is a system in which all learners achieve, gaining new knowledge, understanding and skills through stimulating and expert subject teaching. Programmes will be tailored to individual needs and learners will take responsibility for their learning. Support services such as guidance, counselling and libraries will be accessible, professional and attuned to the needs of learners. Teaching and training will be inspiring, based on imaginative resources and led by subject and sectoral experts who are also skilled teachers or trainers. More and more learners will be following programmes delivered by providers that specialise in that subject area.

1.14 The system will attract high quality staff at all levels and give them excellent opportunities for progression and continuing development. They will be respected for their subject expertise and professionalism, and valued by employers and learners alike. Senior managers will be expert in leading quality review, assurance and improvement. The benefits of technology will be fully exploited, supporting innovation and creativity in teaching and learning. Each college or provider will see quality as at the core of its business and be constantly striving for improvement.

1.15 As a result, the system will have a reputation for high and rising standards. Young people and adults will want to participate, because they will be confident that their learning and qualifications will help them achieve their own goals and ambitions. Employers will be impressed by the commitment to quality of service, and be able to find education and training that adds real value to their business.

1.16 In this White Paper, we set out a programme of change in FE to deliver this vision and meet the demands of the Leitch review and 14-19 reforms, in six key areas:

- strengthening the focus of the system as a whole on a core economic mission, with increasing specialisation in colleges, so that right across the sector all providers are developing distinctive specialist excellence;
- a greater focus within that mission on meeting the needs and demands of learners and employers;
- ensuring that the quality of teaching and learning is uniformly excellent across the sector, with programmes that are well tailored to the needs of individual students;
- a more robust framework of intervention and support to tackle poor quality and promote a diverse range of good providers;
- a reconfiguration of the funding and organisation of the sector to meet these priorities; and
- a new relationship with colleges and other providers, so that they are freed from unnecessary burdens and supported to deliver.

1.17 The next six chapters of this White Paper set out our plans in each of these areas in turn. The final chapter then describes the overall impact of these plans, for learners, employers and providers.

1.18 This White Paper covers the whole Further Education and training system. Its main focus is the role and operation of publicly funded colleges and training providers. The document makes clear where proposals are relevant to other parts of the system, including school sixth forms, providers of Adult and Community Learning, independent training providers and training in the workplace.

1.19 This White Paper applies to England only and is accompanied by a technical supplement, and a point by point response to Sir Andrew Foster's recommendations, which can be found at www.dfes.gov.uk/furthereducation. We intend to move rapidly to implementation, to build on the recent track record of improvement in the system, through a dedicated joint programme between the Department for Education and Skills (DfES) and the LSC, overseen by a Ministerial Group.

1.20 We must count upon the continued effort and commitment of all parts of the system to drive this forward. We will also continue to work closely with employers and unions. These reforms reflect the extensive consultation already undertaken by Ministers and officials, but we welcome further comments and views. If you would like to comment, please contact us by Friday 30 June 2006 at:

Consultation Unit
Department for Education and Skills
Area 2A
Castle View House
East Lane
Runcorn
Cheshire
WA7 2GJ

Or by email to fe.reform@dfes.gsi.gov.uk

Chapter 2: A specialised system focused on employability

A clear mission for FE, focused on the employability and progression of learners, is central to delivering the skills and qualifications which individuals, employers and the economy need.

The delivery of this new mission will involve the creation of a new specialist system. We will expect every FE provider to develop one or more areas of specialist excellence, which will become central to the mission and ethos of the institution and will drive improvement throughout it. The programme of Centres of Vocational Excellence (CoVEs) will be central to this – with a new, higher standard for accreditation and stronger encouragement to develop several CoVEs in related disciplines within a single institution. New, national sector-based networks of vocational providers led by National Skills Academies will be increasingly important in driving improvement.

Recognising its existing specialisation, we will promote a stronger and growing Sixth Form College sector. The wider FE system has a crucial role in delivering our 14-19 reform programme and Sixth Form Colleges particularly so. Sixth Form Colleges will increasingly broaden the curriculum and qualifications they offer as part of 14-19 reform, and will offer some courses to 14-16 year olds. We will recognise particularly effective provision in Sixth Form Colleges through a new 'Centre of Excellence' designation.

This economic mission does not mean narrow vocationalism. It includes for instance the general education that employers value and the stepping stone provision that helps prepare people for success in life and work as well as provision at Levels 2 and 3. We will strengthen the role of colleges and training providers in providing HE programmes linked to their economic and social mission.

2.1 The learning and skills sector delivers a wide range of learning and training opportunities to meet the varied needs of individuals, employers and communities. It is genuinely comprehensive, providing opportunities at levels from basic skills through to HE, and for all ages from 14 upwards. We remain committed to a broad range of provision. One of the sector's strengths has been its ability to respond quickly to new and changing local and national priorities.

2.2 But this strength also presents significant challenges. Many employers and prospective learners find it difficult to navigate this complexity, making it harder for the sector to build a reputation for distinctive excellence. The breadth can also impact on the quality of provision.

2.3 We therefore seek a significantly different system. Its focus will be on those areas of learning where the distinctive strengths of FE can have the biggest impact on progression, life chances and opportunity and hence the biggest impact on the economy and society. Such a system will be based upon institutions with distinctive, specialist strengths, offering in those areas of strength a quality of education and training unrivalled anywhere.

The mission of the FE system will be more clearly focused on the skills and attributes needed for employment

2.4 We agree with Sir Andrew Foster that the key strategic role for the sector – the role in which the contribution of FE to learners' lives, to society and the economy can exceed that of any other part of the education and training system – is to help people gain the skills and qualifications for employability, so that they are equipped for productive, sustainable and fulfilling employment in a modern economy. The qualifications learners gain in FE should be beneficial in themselves and should support individuals to enter, and progress in, the labour market. FE has the leading role to play in helping both young people and adults to acquire the skills which are an essential component of a competitive economy and to develop their careers whilst they are in work, including for the self-employed. This purpose must be central and must be achieved to world class standard.

2.5 Through this document, we set out a range of measures that will contribute to this focus. It will inform all our decisions about which courses should be the priority for funding; and decisions about withdrawing from provision that is not up to standard. It will inform decisions about the deployment of capital resources to develop and improve the FE estate. It will inform the ways in which we seek to support colleges and other providers to improve their provision.

2.6 We are also configuring the infrastructure supporting colleges and other providers to develop this focus. Reforms to qualifications for young people and adults will make sure that colleges are able to focus their resources on delivering qualifications (both general and vocational) which are central to this mission. The progression pathways created by these new qualifications will enable the system to discharge its mission – to develop learners' skills and knowledge to ever higher levels, including through the provision of HE.

2.7 Specialisation will also be supported by the evolving Skills for Business Network. Supported by the Sector Skills Development Agency (SSDA), there are now 25 employer-led Sector Skills Councils (SSCs), covering 85% of the UK workforce. The SSCs and Sector Skills Agreements (SSAs) provide a strong mechanism to ensure that employers, sector by sector, can shape the training provided by the system, helping also to ensure a continued focus on what will be of most value to learners. New structural models such as Trusts and federations and strong networks between specialist providers will help to spread effective practice. Regulatory bodies will also play an important role in shaping training in appropriate sectors, such as Health and Social Care.

2.8 This mission is not narrowly about occupationally-specific training, nor only about training people to Level 2, as the threshold for employability, centrally important though both of these are. It also extends to broad vocational and general qualifications, often valued most of all by employers. It includes fostering an enterprise culture and, for young people in particular, it must extend to inculcating the values, attitudes and knowledge that society seeks from its citizens. It extends from supporting learners to acquire basic skills right through to degree-level education and training to develop very high-level skills, and includes the needs of the self-employed.

2.9 We also recognise that this mission for the system will mean different things to different providers. We believe that greater specialisation will be an important means of delivering the mission. Some colleges are of course already specialist – such as those focusing on agriculture or art and design. And a general FE college which is one amongst several in a city faces different choices to one which is the sole provider in a medium-sized town. It will still be for each governing body to determine its own direction.

Institutions in the FE system will become more specialised

2.10 We believe that real specialisation can make a major contribution to the quality of provision. We want a far higher proportion of learners to be learning in truly excellent specialist provision. But specialisation can be more than that: it should also help to define an institution's distinctive mission and contribution, provide a focus for engaging employers, and create an impetus for improvement and excellence across the organisation.

Every FE institution will develop specialist excellence

2.11 It is our ambition that every organisation in the FE system should develop a distinctive mission, linked to one or more areas of specialist excellence. Already, there are many forms of specialisation in the sector: specialist colleges working in a single defined area; and Sixth Form Colleges, centres and school sixth forms, specialising in learning for 16-19 year-olds. Centres of Vocational Excellence (CoVEs) are an existing form of specialisation, typically in more broadly-based institutions.

2.12 We will build on these existing forms of specialisation. But it is our ambition to move further – towards a truly specialised system. We want specialisation to be about more than a single centre of excellence. It should affect the ethos and mission of the entire institution, become a lever for wider improvement across the college or provider and become part of the identity of the institution.

2.13 As the LSC continues to implement its policy of 'buying quality', a growing proportion of provision will come to be concentrated in the institutions most capable of delivering it effectively, so that ever higher proportions of learners are learning in excellent, specialised provision. This will not be a blanket, undifferentiated policy – the LSC's approach will continue to reflect the needs of local areas and the need to avoid geographical gaps in provision. And there will remain an important role for large, general FE colleges serving a wide range of community needs. These will develop one or more areas of specialist excellence. Such specialisation will better meet the needs of employers and learners, raise the profile of and broaden the recruitment base for particular employment sectors, and enable stronger networks of practice – with leading providers sharing expertise.

A broader and more challenging standard for Centres of Vocational Excellence will drive specialisation

2.14 The CoVE programme has been our main means of promoting specialisation and excellence. Since 2001, a total of 403 CoVEs have been identified. An inspectorate survey in spring 2005 concluded that CoVEs have made an important contribution to raising the profile and status of vocational education and training. Progress has been made in increasing learner numbers, identifying skill needs, working with employers and developing specialist facilities. Pilot CoVEs for Entrepreneurship are due to start later this year.

2.15 We want to build on this and strengthen the programme in a number of ways. First, we want the programme to have a strong focus on improvement across the whole institution. Therefore, the CoVE standard will be changed so that institutions must demonstrate how CoVE status will play a part in defining the mission and purpose of the institution and in driving improvement across the whole institution. Second, if this is to be achieved, there must be effective leadership and management of the institution as a whole and no areas of significant weakness – so this will become a second criterion for CoVE status. The outcomes and impact achieved by the institution will be an important element of the assessment.

2.16 Third, we want there to be real concentrations of CoVEs in related disciplines in individual institutions. This will contribute to a drive towards specialisation, increase the clarity of focus in the institution and create critical mass so that the combined effect of the CoVEs can be significant improvement across the institution. The LSC's planning and funding powers as well as the criteria for CoVE status will make sure that there are clear incentives to develop such concentrations of CoVEs in order to create specialist institutions.

2.17 Finally, we will make excellence in working with employers a key criterion, including responsiveness to employer and sector skill needs. We will also draw on SSC and Regional Skills Partnership advice about the skills priorities in each sector and region in making judgements on CoVE status. And we will raise awareness, particularly amongst employers, of what specialist providers have to offer.

2.18 The LSC will work with SSCs, other employer organisations and providers to develop in detail a new standard drawing on these key elements. The new standard will be used both to accredit the next generation of CoVEs and when we redesignate existing CoVEs – so over time, all CoVEs will need to meet this standard. It will strengthen and replace the current CoVE standard. It will also build upon the Quality Mark proposals for employer responsiveness set out in the LSC's *agenda for change* so that there will be a single standard for recognising excellence at subject or sector level. We are deliberately and significantly raising the bar of quality and performance to extend the best of what has been achieved so far.

2.19 The LSC will trial the new standard through to the autumn, and roll out the new system from the end of 2006. Those gaining accreditation will have priority access to capital funding. They will be strongly placed to win LSC funds and will have a competitive advantage, for instance, in attracting Train to Gain business from employers.

Specialisation in Birmingham

An LSC review of construction provision in Birmingham and Solihull, in response to significant growth and regeneration activity in the area, identified that provision was incapable of meeting the need for over 5,000 additional skilled craftspeople and that there was a demand for up-skilling in the key occupational areas of trowel trades, carpentry and joinery, electrical and gas. Training facilities were inadequate in size, scale and quality with significant difficulties in recruiting good quality trainers and teaching staff.

A decision was taken to consolidate provision within a number of key providers and establish a new purpose built Construction Centre. Two large local FE providers transferred all their general craft construction provision to the £18.5 million Construction Centre at South Birmingham College whilst retaining specialist electrical engineering and gas training. The Centre's capacity for 2,500 full time learners represents a 40% growth in available provision within Birmingham and Solihull. The Centre offers professional qualifications up to degree level and NVQ courses up to Level 3 for bricklayers, electricians, plumbers, plasterers and roofers. A 60% increase in enrolments has enabled the Centre to increase the number of staff and respond quickly and positively to immediate local needs. It has trained over 200 former employees of MG Rover on intensive programmes.

The review that took place in Birmingham and Solihull has been extended to construction provision across the whole region. A regional specialist provision network involving the LSC in partnership with SummitSkills and CITB and all regional CoVEs has been established to take forward its findings, and improve the responsiveness of construction provision across the West Midlands.

New National Skills Academies will drive specialist networks

2.20 In the new, specialised system we seek, networks of specialist institutions will become increasingly strong drivers of the system. Highly effective providers, well engaged with employers, will play an increasing role in developing and disseminating effective practice. Such networks will play a particular role in wider 14-19 learning networks in supporting a wide range of institutions, including schools as well as colleges and other providers, to deliver the new specialised Diplomas. They can also help to ensure that the FE sector understands employer needs fully and can contribute to workforce development.

2.21 National Skills Academies (NSAs) can play a leading role in driving these networks. Proposals for NSAs will be led by employers, who will be sponsors, with the support of SSCs. NSAs will deliver high quality training by establishing national centres of excellence in skills and training for the major sectors of the economy. We plan to establish twelve NSAs by 2008. They will provide a hub for the development and delivery of high quality vocational and occupational learning in their specialism. They will have a leading role in sharing the latest industry best practice in training design and identifying relevant qualifications. We invited the first round of proposals for NSAs in July 2005, and the first four successful bids were announced in October 2005: Construction; Manufacturing; Financial Services; and Food and Drink.

National Manufacturing Skills Academy

The National Manufacturing Skills Academy will create a curriculum of globally competitive training and education in best practice manufacturing techniques, which will progressively be made available to all companies involved in manufacturing in the UK. A key focus will be building UK capability to achieve global competitiveness and raise productivity.

The Academy will be the single point of contact and focus for the brokerage, design and delivery of high quality flexible training provision in the key areas of technical workforce development and management and leadership. Administration and technical content will be controlled at a national hub, with delivery at or near to the place of work, in spokes located in each region.

Employers currently involved include Rolls Royce, BAe, Cobham, Ford, Toyota, Nissan and Filtronics Components, working with SEMTA (the Science, Engineering, Manufacturing Technologies Alliance). Initially, the Academy will focus on four sub-sectors (aerospace, automotive, electronics and marine) but over time will grow to cover the whole sector.

2.22 We are publishing the prospectus for the second round of NSAs alongside this White Paper. Proposals are due to be submitted by June 2006. As resources allow, we will keep building the network, to achieve at least one National Skills Academy for each major sector.

2.23 The specialist, sector-based networks will bring together colleges, CoVEs, specialist departments in HE, independent training providers, and vocational specialist schools. They will play a part in improving the responsiveness, quality and delivery of adult and employer-led training, in the effective delivery of 14-19 specialised Diplomas and in supporting the delivery of Foundation Degrees. We expect these networks to become increasingly important elements of a self-improving system as the system becomes more specialised. They will also help raise awareness of their sectors and overcome stereotyping and other social and cultural barriers to entry.

We will strengthen our support for institutions focusing on young people as part of 14-19 reform

2.24 Other institutions specialise in provision for young people rather than in a subject area, and these too have a key role to play in delivering the 14-19 reforms. We want that part of the sector focusing on provision for 16-19 year-olds to be strong and growing, to ask it to expand its remit in delivering 14-19 reform and to recognise specialist excellence as it does so. School sixth forms also play an important part in delivering for 16-19 year-olds and already benefit from the opportunity to take on a specialism, as part of the wider specialism of the school. All of the work of schools, colleges and other providers will be set in the context of locally agreed strategies. We do not expect any single institution acting alone, to deliver the full statutory entitlement. All institutions will need to work together to offer more between them than any could acting alone.

We will expand the Sixth Form College sector

2.25 Sixth Form Colleges and 16-19 schools offer a distinctive form of specialism within the FE system. They often concentrate on A level programmes, but some also play an important role in widening post-16 participation among those not yet ready for study at Level 3 and in offering progression routes to that level. For many in the 16-19 age group they combine the attractions of studying in the more adult environment of a college with a focus on A levels and high rates of progression to university.

2.26 We agree with Sir Andrew Foster and Ofsted that Sixth Form Colleges are a successful and well respected part of the FE sector. They exemplify the benefits of a clear, focused mission which creates shared expectations of high achievement and motivates both staff and learners to give of their best. Tertiary colleges likewise make an important contribution.

2.27 We want a strong and growing Sixth Form College sector. We want it to be easier to establish new Sixth Form Colleges and easier for existing colleges to expand, especially to deliver specialised Diplomas as part of 14-19 reform. In recent years, funding advantages have seen 16-19 schools established, rather than Sixth Form Colleges. We see the two types of institution as taking essentially the same role within the system. We have set out elsewhere our intention to narrow the funding gap which can create incentives to establish one type of institution rather than the other.

2.28 Where new 16-19 provision is needed in an area, including cases where a competition is held, a new Sixth Form College should be considered as one option. We set out later in this document our plans for an 'FE presumption', which will make it easier for high performing colleges to expand their 16-19 provision in order to deliver Diplomas, supported by capital grant where this is needed to underpin new provision. Reform of the allocation of capital funding will also create a more level playing field where a new or expanded Sixth Form College is the right solution to local needs.

We will ask 16-19 institutions to take a broader role in 14-19 reform and recognise Centres of Excellence

2.29 As part of local partnership arrangements, Sixth Form Colleges (as well as other FE providers) will have a significant role to play in 14-19 reform. We want Sixth Form Colleges to offer specialised Diplomas, including at Level 3 as a strong preparation for progression into HE. We also think that they can play a part in delivering to 14-16 year-olds in Key Stage 4 who are on the roll of local schools. This could include providing opportunities for more stretching options and acceleration and the delivery of Diplomas to this age group.

2.30 There are a few Sixth Form Colleges which have achieved CoVE status, as a result of delivering highly effective vocational provision. We welcome this. However, we also recognise that for some Sixth Form Colleges, CoVE status would not be an appropriate reflection of their curriculum – and nor, of course, are they eligible for specialist school status.

2.31 We therefore intend to develop and consult on a new 'Centre of Excellence' standard, which will recognise excellence in delivery for 16-19 year-olds, linked to the CoVE framework but without the same vocational emphasis. As with the new CoVE standard, we will develop a demanding standard, intended to recognise truly effective practice and good leadership and management and to promote the improvement of the whole institution. We want particularly to recognise those institutions making a significant contribution to delivery of a local 14-19 strategy.

2.32 As recommended by Sir Andrew Foster, we will ensure a distinctive policy focus within DfES and the LSC on the Sixth Form Colleges group, to understand their particular needs and work with them to implement these proposals.

Within the new system, the range of provision will remain broad

2.33 We are clear that within the new mission of the system and the new focus on specialisation, we need to retain breadth of provision. This applies to the system as a whole and, where appropriate, to individual institutions.

'Skills and employability' is a broad mission – and includes the general education employers value and stepping stone provision

2.34 Within this renewed economic focus, there is clearly an important role for both vocational and general learning, which many providers already combine very successfully. The new specialised Diplomas will require a combination of theoretical and practical learning. In considering how to deliver its mission effectively, each provider will continue to decide for itself the right balance of courses to offer. In every case, there should be a considered and deliberate overarching concern to promote the life chances and employability of learners.

2.35 This strong focus on economic impact does not come at the expense of social inclusion and equality of opportunity – the two reinforce one another. The sector as a whole is uniquely well-placed to provide opportunities for second-chance learning and personal development. These opportunities are often the essential precursors to success in adult and working life, and to career development. We must sustain and strengthen stepping stone programmes, to encourage re-entry to learning. We describe in this White Paper how we will improve opportunity in this area through creating the Foundation Learning Tier. Many colleges and providers do excellent work to provide access to learning for young people in difficult circumstances. DfES will work with the Department for Work and Pensions (DWP) to improve support for this group. Colleges also play an invaluable role in promoting community cohesion and integration, providing settings where young people and adults from every ethnic, faith and social group can come together. Many colleges are exemplars in the diversity of their students and staff, serving as a resource that is available to, and valued by, all sections of their community. We will continue to support colleges in this vital work, and will continue to work with the Home Office on our shared agenda of community renewal, including through the Active Learning for Active Citizens network.

2.36 The Skills for Life national strategy for adult literacy, numeracy and language will continue to be central to tackling the weaknesses in basic skills which can prevent millions of young people and adults from succeeding in life. There will be a renewed drive to improve the quality of this kind of provision. Similarly, our recent Green Paper *Reducing Re-Offending through Skills and Employment* set out how we will raise the skills levels of offenders. This will both contribute to the economy and help break the cycle of criminality which is harmful to individual offenders, their families and society at large.

2.37 Although many forms of provision are fully within the new mission of the sector, we continue to be clear that getting young people and adults to a first, full Level 2 is a vital part – as the minimum platform for employment. Colleges have a leading role in ensuring that as many people as possible achieve their first full Level 2 – a crucial objective for our economy, and for the life chances of countless individuals. This year, Ministers will lead a major campaign to raise the profile of this national priority area.

2.38 In order to meet our wider employment and pensions strategies, we must raise the employment rate among older workers. Opportunities for older workers to learn new skills in a changing labour market are therefore essential. DfES and DWP will work together to consider how older workers can be better supported to stay in work.

Foundation Degrees and HE in FE will continue to grow in importance

2.39 FE colleges and training providers already play an important and distinctive part in HE, and within the focus on employability, there will be an important and growing role for this provision. Some 10% of all HE learners are studying in FE colleges and more than 50% of them are part-time compared with about 35% in HE as a whole. Some 25,000 learners in colleges are studying on Foundation Degree programmes, designed and delivered in partnership with employers, to give a strong foundation for employment in a chosen sector.

2.40 In line with the wider mission, there should be a presumption that HE delivered in FE should have a strong occupational and employment purpose. The major area of expansion will be Foundation Degrees. We will also expand work-based HE programmes. In the next chapter we set out major new proposals for FE colleges and training providers to play an important part in that, working within the Train to Gain framework to offer integrated training programmes for, and co-financed with, employers, ranging from basic skills to HE.

2.41 We will also develop centres of HE excellence in FE colleges, focused on the twin themes of employability and widening participation. We have asked the Higher Education Funding Council for England (HEFCE) to treat these as high priorities for funding allocations. Equally, where colleges are not delivering to the right standard, HE provision should not continue. Not all FE colleges are well placed to deliver HE, and we will ask the HEFCE to review the effectiveness of small pockets of HE in FE colleges.

2.42 FE is particularly effective in providing HE for learners from more disadvantaged groups, backgrounds and communities. Many FE colleges offer flexible, local opportunities which make HE accessible to people who might otherwise face significant barriers to participation. The sector is well placed to promote wider participation in HE. The HEFCE has recently announced additional funding of £12 million to support widening participation in 2006-07.

2.43 We believe that FE has an important role to play in areas currently without any HE provision, and will continue to support the development of lifelong learning networks (LLNs). These combine the strengths of a number of diverse providers and allow sharing of teaching expertise, curricula and facilities. They enable learners to move between different kinds of vocational and academic programmes, and between institutions, as their interests, needs and abilities develop. There are currently ten such networks in operation, covering over 40 universities and 100 FE colleges, and expansion of LLNs will be a priority in future years. The HEFCE and the LSC will identify priority areas where provision is currently most sparse, with a view to starting LLNs in these areas by September 2008.

2.44 To ensure funding supports these developments, we have asked the HEFCE and the LSC to explore mechanisms for further capital support to enable FE providers to contribute to HE, including direct funding of HE facilities in FE colleges. We have also asked them to review the financial arrangements that underpin HE courses in FE colleges, including franchising arrangements. It is important that money should follow the learner in ways that are transparent and build confidence.

Wider activity will continue

2.45 A clear focus on employability does not mean we will stop all other activity. Alongside the core economic mission, we remain strongly committed to learning for personal fulfilment, civic participation and community development, and are taking steps to strengthen the range and quality of such provision. We have allocated £210 million in 2006-07 for personal and community development learning (PCDL), and we will maintain this level of funding in 2007-08. But there will increasingly be an expectation that individuals should pay for this kind of provision where they can afford to do so.

PCDL provision in Liverpool

Liverpool City Council provides a well-equipped mobile learning centre which aims to engage learners in the most deprived wards of the city. It works with a range of organisations including care homes and mental health charities. Delivery is flexible to allow for the needs of all learners. Older learners in a sheltered residential setting, for example, have shortened sessions over a longer time period.

So far nearly 2,000 people have used the centre. It has also been involved in Adult Learners' Week, healthy eating campaigns and promoting opportunities in Higher Education. Engagement with one mental health charity has resulted in seven learners attending IT courses. Feedback from learners indicates that they like the mobile centre coming to them, the friendly atmosphere and the fact that it does not look like a classroom.

2.46 We will reinvigorate this type of learning through local LSC Partnerships, which look beyond just LSC funded learning and include a wide range of recreational, health-related and cultural learning funded through other sources. We want representatives of learners, including voluntary and community groups, as well as providers, to plan provision in a co-ordinated and cost effective way in line with local community priorities.

2.47 We will continue to assess the effectiveness and impact of the 28 Testbed Learning Communities (TLCs) established as a result of the 2003 White Paper *21st Century Skills.* TLCs have developed innovative ways of introducing people to the study skills relevant to progression to vocational qualifications. The lessons learnt from their experience will feed into the work being done by the LSC and through the National Institute of Adult and Continuing Education (NIACE) and others to establish effective local modes of delivery for PCDL.

2.48 The pattern of institutions providing these opportunities may change as funding is directed to those most capable of delivering effectively. We would expect the balance to continue to shift away from general FE colleges as they focus more sharply on their core mission. We expect that, in time, some providers, often in the voluntary and community sectors, will want to specialise in this type of provision. We would also expect that the principles of contestability would apply equally to LSC funded PCDL. There should be opportunities for new providers, for example from the voluntary and community sector, to assist with the revitalisation of this type of learning.

Chapter 3: A system meeting the needs of learners and employers

We will put the needs and priorities of learners and employers at the heart of the system, both to make sure that the FE system delivers its central mission and to continue to incentivise further improvement.

We will introduce measures that will put learners and employers in the driving seat in determining what is funded and how services are delivered. A programme of learner accounts will be trialled, focused on helping people gain Level 3 qualifications. There will be a new entitlement for a first full Level 3 qualification for those aged 19 to 25, supported by an expanded Adult Learning Grant (ALG), new funding for both of which was announced in the Budget on 22 March 2006. The new 19-25 entitlement and national roll-out of ALG will both be implemented from 2007/8, creating a new integrated package of support for young adults continuing their initial education to Level 3.

The Train to Gain programme will be expanded, so that more adult training is delivered in the workplace through programmes designed and delivered in partnership with employers. The programme will also be widened to provide access to HE level skills and courses. Sector Skills Agreements will become the key mechanism to ensure that employer needs and priorities shape the supply of education and training, and secure increased demand and investment.

This will be underpinned by qualification reform which ensures better progression routes for young people (through specialised Diplomas) and greater simplicity and navigability for adults.

3.1 A system which focuses on employability and aims to support the future success of young people and adult learners will be one which responds more and more sharply to the needs and demands of its customers – learners and employers. Creating a system where these demands are more easily heard and where there are clear incentives to act on them will not only mean that FE is discharging its mission more fully, but will create incentives for improvement and opportunities to expand to meet employer needs.

3.2 FE has a good record of reaching out to those who are difficult to engage. Nonetheless, if we are to meet the skill demands of future economic growth and employment, then we need to increase the demand from employers and potential learners and address the cultural, social and economic factors which can limit aspiration and participation. We have to engage not only those learners and employers who already see how skills and qualifications can help them, but the millions who regard education and training as having nothing of value to offer them.

The system will focus more closely on meeting the needs of learners

3.3 We will enable learners to choose the programmes that will best help them to achieve their goals, in the setting that is right for them, and we will make the system more responsive to those choices.

We will create a new entitlement to remove financial barriers for 19-25 year-olds

3.4 We propose to introduce a new entitlement to free tuition for a first full Level 3 qualification for 19 to 25 year-olds from 2007-08, supported by an extra £25 million from Budget 2006. This will help us to tackle an area of particular weakness in skills development in this country. In many other countries, much larger numbers of young adults achieve Level 2 and 3 qualifications between the ages of 19 and 25. In this country, by contrast, there is at present a sharp divide at the age of 19. Up until that age, every young person who wants to participate in education and training, full time or part time, is guaranteed free access. Beyond 19, there is a clear, well-understood pathway for young people who have achieved a Level 3 qualification and want to progress into HE. They are well supported to carry on in initial education through to the age of 21 or 22.

3.5 For those who do not get to Level 3 and go on to HE, the options for continuing in their late teens and early twenties can be less clear. The new entitlement for a first full Level 3 for 19 to 25 year-olds builds on the existing entitlement to free tuition towards a first full Level 2 qualification (equivalent to 5 GCSEs at grades A* – C). To support the introduction of this new entitlement, we will expect all Sector Qualifications Strategies to identify the full Level 3 programmes that employers in that sector judge most valuable, so that we can inform and advise learners accordingly. That will include promoting advanced Apprenticeships.

3.6 This new entitlement will give many more young adults an opportunity to prepare themselves for success in life through the education and training system. It will improve our skills base and help us to close the gap between qualification levels in this country and abroad, which opens up in this age group. It will provide routes back for those who left education early and want to return in order to improve their qualifications and job prospects. Evidence tells us that it will particularly benefit disadvantaged young adults. As set out below, we aim to extend this entitlement over time and as resources allow, so that it can include programmes within the Foundation Learning Tier that support progression through to Level 2 and beyond.

New learning accounts will hand power to learners

3.7 We will introduce a new system of learner accounts for adult learners. We know that giving learners greater choice and control over their learning energises people and gives them a real sense of empowerment. The account will hold virtual funds, which can be used to pay for learning at the discretion of the learner. It can have a life extending over a period of time and can hold funds from the state, the learner and the employer. It will be administered by a third party and made robust by the development of the Unique Learner Number.

3.8 Accounts could be used in principle for all education costs. But they work best where there is an informed and demanding customer group, able and motivated to exercise real choice. So we propose to test the concept with adult learners studying for a Level 3 qualification, as a further way of tackling our relative skills gaps at that level, increasing choice and generating demand for higher level learning from non-traditional groups. We expect Union Learning Representatives and Information, Advice and Guidance (IAG) advisers to play a significant role in steering many individuals to the course that will best meet their needs.

How we expect accounts to work

Learners will become account holders on achieving a first full Level 2, on enrolling for a Level 3 course, or on being recommended for a full Level 3 course by an Information Advice and Guidance adviser or Union Learning Representative.

On becoming an account holder, the learner will receive a membership card and an account number. They will be entitled to a discount on the cost of a Level 3 course at any LSC sponsored provider, with the discount set to reflect the national fee rate set by the LSC for that year (37.5% fees and 62.5% public funding subsidy in 2007-8). For 19-25 year-olds, under the new entitlement, provision will, of course, be free. The new adult guidance service will offer expert advice on choosing a provider, drawing up a learning plan, on career development and on financial support, including the Adult Learning Grant and how to access financial help with childcare.

Shortly after enrolment on a course, the learner will receive their first account statement that sets out their own financial contribution, the state's financial contribution, Adult Learning Grant, learner support, if any, and other financial contributions, for example from their employer.

3.9 In the trials of accounts, the state will make a contribution to the overall costs at the level that reflects the national fee rate applying in that year, except where accounts are used to deliver the new 19-25 entitlement, where the costs will be met in full. IAG services will make sure that learners completing a Level 2 course know that the Level 3 account is the next step on from the Level 2 entitlement; and Union Learning Representatives (ULRs) will help their members access and use accounts.

3.10 We are very conscious in taking this step of the problems that have marred previous similar initiatives. Having analysed the lessons from those problems, we believe that they can be avoided in the management of this scheme. Strong quality assurance of providers through an LSC approval process will prevent unscrupulous operators taking advantage of it. There will be careful evaluation of the pilot before decisions are taken about expansion: the LSC will trial accounts from autumn 2007. And payments will be made through the existing well-tested payments system, not through a new, bespoke arrangement. In taking forward these proposals, we will draw on the experience of accounts programmes that have been developed in other countries, including Switzerland, the Netherlands and Spain.

Learners will be more involved in decisions

3.11 We know that when learners participate in decisions affecting their learning experience, they are likely to play a more active role in the provider's quality improvement process. Equally, the involvement of some learners can directly improve the responsiveness of the system to the concerns of learners more generally. We will encourage more learner representation in all aspects of the system – from national policymaking to course content and delivery.

3.12 A National Learner Panel and the direct involvement of learners in national and local agencies will increase their influence in key policy decisions. Colleges and training providers will be expected to develop and implement strategies for involving learners and parents/carers of younger learners. We expect learners to play a key role in institutional governance, with each governing body including at least two learner governors. Based on the LSC national learner satisfaction survey, there should be regular opportunities for learners to feed back their levels of satisfaction so that colleges and providers can make improvements. And there should be effective mechanisms for engaging with learners collectively, including through student committees. We will work with the LSC and Ofsted to ensure that these mechanisms are reflected in development plans.

3.13 Working with the Centre for Excellence in Leadership, the Association of Colleges and the National Union of Students we will extend the successful national scheme of support for learner representatives. And we will strengthen the Staff Student Liaison Officer type role by asking Lifelong Learning UK (LLUK) to develop standards for this vital role.

3.14 Opportunities to undertake volunteering activities can enrich the learning experience in FE and promote active citizenship. Volunteering can enable students to develop the soft skills required by employers, strengthen providers' engagement with their local communities and help foster an inclusive ethos.

We will ensure that employers can get what they want and need

3.15 Alongside learners, employers are the major customers of FE. We have already made huge strides in putting employer needs at the heart of the FE system. We have now established the full network of 25 SSCs, led by employers to ensure that their needs and priorities for the skills that will support productivity are both articulated through SSAs and met through more responsive provision. SSCs are playing a central role in designing the new specialised Diplomas for 14-19 year-olds. SSCs have made an important contribution to focusing public funding in FE on the priorities.

The new Train to Gain programme will make the system more responsive to employers

3.16 From April 2006, the new national programme for adult learners, Train to Gain, will deliver training, normally in the workplace, designed and delivered to suit the employer's operational needs. A network of impartial brokers will help employers to assess their training needs and find suitable training for employees to meet those needs. Basic skills and first, full Level 2 provision will remain a priority and be free; Level 3 provision in the two trial regions (North West and West Midlands) will receive a state contribution of up to 50% of the costs; and new trials of HE level skills will be subsidised. Employers will be able to use the brokers to find a comprehensive training package. Brokers will focus their time on those employers, employees and sectors that have historically not engaged in training, and where the Women and Work Commission has identified a problem for female workers in particular. They will not interfere in established training relationships which are working well, but will make new matches between employers and providers. Their work will be integrated with wider business support services managed by Regional Development Agencies. The funding allocated is £288 million for 2006-07 and £457 million for 2007-08.

Train to Gain – an illustration

Peter, Tariq and Amber work for a small employer who was keen get some additional training for her staff. A skills broker working through the Train to Gain service got in touch with the manager to gain an understanding of the company's development needs, identified who would benefit from learning and developed a training plan. The broker identified a choice of providers to deliver the different courses required and the manager chose the local college as the best option for price, delivery and location of the training i.e. in the workplace. The college assessed each learner's training needs.

Amber took a Level 2 NVQ in business administration so she could take on more of the administrative work and manage the office systems better. Tariq agreed to undertake a technician course at Level 3. Peter left school over 25 years ago with no formal qualifications. He took a basic skills course to provide him with the essential skills in reading and maths that he missed at school, and will look to progress to a Level 2 qualification later.

A few months after the training was completed, the broker followed up to assess how everything had gone. The manager was pleased that the training got underway quickly without waiting for a new term to start, and that the provider was flexible in response to the demands of the business. Early results from the training included improved office systems as Amber took on more work and became more efficient. In the warehouse, where Peter works, errors fell from 15% to 10%, resulting in a much lower rate of return from dissatisfied customers. The manager has asked for a further skills assessment to be carried out with the other warehouse staff.

3.17 Importantly, we will also begin to offer skills development at HE level through this service. Starting in September 2006 we will extend the Train to Gain service so that employers in three pathfinder regions can meet their skill needs at Level 4 and above through Train to Gain brokers, as well as through their direct links with HE institutions. FE colleges and HE institutions, in partnership with SSCs, RDAs and employers in priority regional economic sectors, will establish new, flexible workplace focused skills provision centred on the needs of employers and employees. This will enable employees with Level 3 qualifications or below to progress to HE level qualifications. Because of the potentially high returns to employers and employees, they will be expected to contribute significantly to co-financing customised provision alongside the Government's contribution. We will monitor take-up carefully, including the impact on access to training for ethnic minorities and other groups currently under-represented in work based training.

3.18 In addition, as a result of Budget 2006, a further £10 million in each of the next two years will be made available for a new Level 3 skills Train to Gain pilot. This will focus on low-skilled, part time and ethnic minority women, in order to tackle the barriers these women may face in the labour market. This forms part of a £20 million per annum package to respond to the Women and Work Commission's recent report, recommending action to tackle the barriers many women face in the labour market. The other two elements of this package are £5 million per annum to double the number of skills coaching pilots, extending the trials to 11 Jobcentre Plus districts to target support for low-skilled women not in the labour market; and £5 million per annum for the SSDA to work with a number of SSCs for whom representation is a particular issue. By testing new recruitment and career pathways through this initiative we expect to help at least 5,000 women each year.

We will listen to employers and respond to their requirements as set out in Sector Skills Agreements

3.19 In addition to the directly demand-led Train to Gain, we want employer requirements to have a greater role in shaping the supply of education and training for adults more widely. To achieve this, Sector Skills Agreements (SSAs), which will be an agreement between Government and the SSC and employers, will become a key mechanism for determining priorities for the use of public funding for adult training and skills. There will be explicit links between the requirements set out in an SSA and the types of programmes funded (in the case of England) through Train to Gain.

3.20 Each SSA will set out the priorities of that sector for the skills and qualifications that will make most difference to productivity. They will incorporate robust Sector Qualification Strategies that identify which qualifications employers rate as priorities. Where they exist, regulatory bodies will also play a key role in determining sectoral skill requirements, fitness to practise and licence to practise. The agreement will drive LSC decisions in each region on the allocation of funds to providers to prioritise those skills and qualifications. Regional Skills Partnerships will play a key part in this decision making process.

3.21 SSAs will also set out the commitments employers themselves are making: investment of funds (for example through voluntary training pools), collective expectations about skills requirements (for example, through voluntary licences to practise), and direct engagement with training providers (for example, in setting up National Skills Academies).

3.22 The second phase of the Leitch review will consider how to raise employers' demand for, and investment in, skills. SSAs can play an important part in this.

We will support colleges to work effectively with employers

3.23 For most general FE colleges and all other training providers, it has long been part of their mission to work with employers in their community and to help their learners gain good employment skills. But recent Ofsted reports have shown that some providers do not approach this systematically. Even in those that are actively engaged in employer training, an overarching strategy is "largely missing"; and the substantial effort being devoted to this area may not be achieving as much as it could.

3.24 So we will support colleges and other training providers to work more effectively with employers. We will ask a range of partners to develop a new good practice framework for providers to consider when setting their own strategy.

3.25 We expect the framework to cover the role of the governing body in leading this work, guidance on how to support local employers more effectively across the range of their work and advice on how best to involve employers directly (particularly in equal opportunities and the delivery of Diplomas, work experience and wider opportunities for 14-19 year-olds). It will also advise colleges and other providers on how to integrate the employer perspective into all their mainstream activities, for example by using employer satisfaction data to drive performance.

3.26 The framework will promote the practice adopted in a number of colleges, who have developed an Employers' Charter, setting out the respective responsibilities of the provider and the employer. Done effectively, a Charter can help to inform employers about the range of services provided locally. The process of creating one can help colleges and training providers to reflect on and refine the quality and scope of their offer to employers.

3.27 We want to work further with colleges to ensure that courses are increasingly available as and when employers and learners need them, both to increase productivity in the workplace and to enhance employment opportunities for workless individuals. Flexibility in offering courses outside traditional college timetables will support our aim of ensuring that the FE system contributes to employability.

3.28 Unions have a growing role in promoting training in the workplace. There are now over 12,000 trained ULRs, who play an important role in giving employees the information and confidence to access training. They have been particularly effective in promoting Skills for Life and Train to Gain opportunities, and union representatives are playing an important role in SSCs.

3.29 With Government support, the TUC is now setting up a Union Learning Academy to strengthen the ULR network. It will aim to ensure a good range of training opportunities are available to employees, promote collective training agreements with employers, and ensure the impact of SSAs is seen in individual workplaces. The TUC is developing proposals for a collective learning fund bringing together resources from learners and employers. We will work with them to consider actively how this might work alongside other initiatives, particularly the learner accounts and Train to Gain proposals set out in this White Paper.

We will create a qualifications system which better serves learners and employers

3.30 As we give learners more control over their own learning experience we need to ensure they are making choices only between valuable options which meet employers' skills requirements and therefore help them succeed and progress.

3.31 The worth of a qualification depends on how widely recognised, understood and valued it is and on how effectively it enables progression in learning and life. General qualifications have always been widely understood and valued and the progression route from GCSE to A level to university is the most well understood and highly regarded educational pathway at present. By contrast, many other qualifications pathways are poorly understood and little valued. There is confusion about the relationships between qualifications, about what particular knowledge and skills are required to achieve certain qualifications and a lack of clarity about progression routes.

3.32 Only when all qualification routes have real currency outside the education system and promote progression within it will the system be able to meet employer and learner needs. Qualification reform is therefore at the heart of our strategy.

Qualifications and curriculum reform for 14-19 year-olds

3.33 In the *14-19 Education and Skills* White Paper, we set out our plans to reform curriculum and qualifications for 11-19 year-olds. At the heart of these proposals is a strong belief that all young people have potential, which should be developed through the education and training system, and that opportunities in the curriculum to learn in different ways will make it more likely that more young people learn and prepare for success in life.

3.34 The Implementation Plan which followed the White Paper in December 2005 set out in detail the reform programme we are now implementing. New specialised Diplomas are being developed by partnerships led by employers and including HE, schools and colleges, as qualifications which can excite and motivate a very wide range of young people, promote and reward practical learning, overcome stereotyping of some sectors and occupations, and develop the wider skills that employers and HE seek. The first five will be available for teaching from 2008. There will be a national entitlement to all 14 Diplomas by 2013. The delivery of this entitlement will require institutions to work together to deliver more between them than they could individually.

3.35 Achieving good basic skills is essential to success in life. Therefore, new functional skills qualifications in English, maths and ICT are being developed, for incorporation into GCSEs, the new specialised Diplomas and Apprenticeships. Locking these into all the qualification routes will provide the strongest possible incentive for young people to achieve the functional skills which are so crucial to later success. Reform of Key Stage 3 will ensure that more young people reach age 14 with the skills and knowledge they need to make a success of upper secondary and post secondary education. More stretching options at advanced level will include a new extended project. Full details are set out in the Implementation Plan.

A new Apprenticeship qualification

3.36 Apprenticeships are one of our best recognised training routes. They have served many people well as a pathway to a successful career in a growing range of sectors. Their distinctiveness comes from their role as a work-based preparation for a particular occupation, designed by employers for that particular occupation and including learning and assessment in occupational competence. As part of our work to strengthen Apprenticeships, we plan to create an Apprenticeship completion award as a recognised qualification. That will help us to drive up the numbers completing Apprenticeships, which are improving fast but remain too low. Often those who do not complete the full framework are completing valuable components of it (such as an NVQ), but we know that completing the full framework has significant benefits to employers (in increased productivity) and Apprentices (in improved career progression and life chances).

3.37 There need to be clear progression routes from specialised Diplomas into Apprenticeships. Apprenticeships will remain distinct and will not be required to fit within the specialised Diploma framework. That would risk losing the crucial requirement that Apprenticeships should be a full preparation for a particular occupation. But it must be easy to move between Apprenticeship programmes and Diplomas at all levels, with full recognition for knowledge and skills already gained. Diploma Development Partnerships will map out progression routes between specialised Diplomas and Apprenticeships and vice versa.

We will simplify qualifications for adults

3.38 We also want vocational qualifications which prepare adult learners better for employment, because they focus on what employers need and are widely understood. We are therefore committed to improving the value and comprehensibility of these qualifications through developing and implementing a 'Framework for Achievement' (FfA) based on units of achievement, which allows learners to build up credit over time towards full qualifications. The goal is to put in place a simpler, clearer structure based on sector qualifications strategies drawn up by SSCs that can provide the basis for qualification developments in the sector.

3.39 These strategies will identify the skills, knowledge and understanding that employers require at different levels for successful employment in the sector. They will identify which combination of units is needed in order to prepare someone for a given trade or occupation. The qualifications identified in this process as meeting the needs of employers in the sector will be located within the FfA, regulated by the Qualifications and Curriculum Authority (QCA), using common definitions of both the level and volume of study. As a result, the current range of existing vocational qualifications will be rationalised to those which best meet employers' needs.

3.40 Following extensive consultation, the QCA will publish a specification for the framework in the spring, and will initiate a period of trialling from September 2006. Work is also underway to establish trial areas. A full report will be produced and submitted to Ministers in the Summer of 2008 to inform decisions about implementation.

We will develop the Foundation Learning Tier for qualifications below Level 2

3.41 It is essential to identify as part of the FfA progression pathways supported by high quality units and qualifications at Entry and Level 1 (including Skills for Life) which will help those who need to progress through manageable and coherent steps get to Level 2 and beyond. So, through the QCA and LSC, working with SSCs, we will develop a framework of well understood, high quality foundation programmes encompassing Entry and Level 1, supported by appropriate qualifications and units from the FfA.

3.42 This coherent framework of provision below Level 2 – the Foundation Learning Tier (FLT) – will replace the present, confusing arrangements. It will allow units and qualifications to be combined in ways that suit the needs and aspirations of the range of learners at this level, including supporting those with learning difficulties to develop the skills to live independently.

3.43 A key driver of the FLT will be the establishment of progression pathways: clear stepping stones to enable learners to access a first full Level 2 programme. These will be supported by accredited units and qualifications from the FfA, developed in line with a clear qualification strategy. In order to promote the understanding and recognition of those programmes which provide progression to Level 2 we have asked the QCA and the LSC to consider what mechanisms can be applied to ensure that Progression Pathways within the FLT can be validated appropriately. We will trial these pathways in 2006/07 and expect to have identified and implemented a full set of progression pathways across the FLT by 2010. Over time, the LSC will concentrate public funds on programmes that align with these pathways; and the new entitlement for 19-25 year-olds will be extended to these programmes as resources allow, so that there is a complete entitlement to progression up to Level 3 for 19-25 year-olds.

Chapter 4: A national strategy for teaching and learning in Further Education

We need a world class education and training system that provides a high quality learning experience for all, making effective use of new technology. Colleges and providers will be responsible for driving up quality within their own organisations, with an increasing emphasis on self-improvement.

For the first time, a single Quality Improvement Agency will be responsible for supporting providers in this role. It will lead the implementation of a single, national Quality Improvement Strategy for teaching and learning in FE. There will be new support for teaching staff in FE, including through the development of new teaching and learning materials, backed by subject coaches, especially in the subject areas of the new specialised Diplomas. The Strategy will support increasing personalisation, so that individual needs and circumstances are built into the design and delivery of education and training.

The Strategy will be backed by new measures to support the development of the workforce. Staff need to be properly trained and to develop and update their skills regularly to respond to changing needs and new challenges. We will introduce a continuing professional development (CPD) requirement, so that staff undertake a minimum amount of CPD each year. With additional funding from Budget 2006, new programmes will be introduced to boost recruitment of talented graduates; encourage highly effective managers from other sectors to come into FE; provide opportunities for skilled specialists to teach in FE; and provide opportunities for FE staff to update their skills in industry. We will also take steps to increase the diversity of the workforce. All new college principals will need to gain the new leadership qualification.

4.1 A clearer mission, a more specialised system and greater responsiveness to learners and employers are all essential if the FE system is to make its maximum contribution to national life, the economy and the opportunities available to learners. Equally important is that the quality of teaching and learning should continue to improve, so that all learners have the best possible opportunities to succeed on their courses. Therefore, a continued drive for quality improvement is at the heart of this White Paper.

For the first time, we will have a single agency and a single strategy for quality improvement

4.2 Responsibility for quality lies with colleges and providers: we seek to get behind their efforts to improve and to make sure that they have access to the best possible support to do so. A new single body, the Quality Improvement Agency (QIA), will bring together the former quality improvement and development activities of the Learning and Skills Development Agency, the DfES Standards and Skills for Life Units, the Learning and Skills Council and the Adult Learning Inspectorate. It will offer a single, integrated approach to quality development and improvement across the sector.

4.3 The QIA will lead the development of that Quality Improvement Strategy (QIS) for the FE sector, which will subsume and build on Success for All. There will be four elements to the QIS: support for quality improvement and workforce development; publication of performance information to drive improvement and enable well-informed choice; intervention where necessary in order to tackle cases where quality is not good enough; and an inspection regime to provide objective, external evidence on quality and standards. The work of the Centre for Excellence in Leadership (CEL) and Lifelong Learning UK (LLUK) will be integrated within the QIS.

4.4 An outline of the QIS will be published in June 2006, with the full Strategy appearing in the autumn. It will be fully operational by April 2007. The Strategy will re-shape national quality improvement activities, building on what works and is valued by colleges and providers, while eliminating overlap and duplication.

4.5 Central to ensuring a high quality, personalised experience for all learners will be support for colleges and providers to develop better teaching and learning practice. The QIA will commission and manage these quality improvement services across the sector, and they will be detailed in a prospectus to be published in April 2006.

4.6 The national teaching and learning change programme for FE will be extended, providing new teaching and learning resources and subject coaching for a priority set of curriculum areas, aligned to the 14-19 specialised Diplomas, and subject coaching networks to enable innovation and sharing of good practice. Specialist subject programmes will be developed to address national shortages in literacy, numeracy and language. There will also be new teaching resources and professional development to support Train to Gain, National Skills Academies and the new Centres of Vocational Excellence.

4.7 Working with the Skills for Business Network, the QIA will support the design and introduction of new, high quality education and training programmes to support achievement of the national targets at Levels 2 and 3, for both young people and adults. This will include advice, training and backup for teachers in the use of the programmes.

4.8 The QIA will develop, by 2008, an 'Excellence Gateway' website bringing together information on quality, currently distributed in many places. It will provide access to self-review and diagnostic tools, planning support and other resources. It will also include a national e-technology support framework to help leaders and senior managers apply technology effectively. Exploiting the benefits that technology can bring to teaching and learning will be critical to our ambition of improving the learner's experience and driving up standards. The website will enable providers to compare their current performance in the effective use of technology with the vision of a provider of the future.

Learning will be more personalised

4.9 The overall objective of the QIS is to support colleges and other providers to offer learners a more personalised experience. The complexity of the FE system can appear daunting and difficult to navigate for learners. The variety of different kinds of learners in different types of provision presents challenges to teachers and trainers in ensuring they teach all their students effectively. We therefore need to support providers to give every learner an experience that really meets their needs: to get them on the right course or programme; to make sure that teaching on that course responds to their needs; and to support them to overcome any barriers to successful completion, where appropriate building on the power of new technology and e-learning to provide personalised approaches.

There will be better guidance

4.10 If learners are to receive truly personalised education and training, then we need to be confident that the system supports them initially to make choices of course and provider which work for them. This means of course that education and training institutions should provide appropriate references for learners whose needs will best be met at other institutions, where necessary. Crucially, it means that we need excellent and impartial IAG services.

4.11 An extensive reform programme is in hand to secure this. We set out in the *Youth Matters* Green Paper and subsequently in the *Next Steps* document our plans for improving IAG for young people. Such improvements are essential to effective implementation of our 14-19 curriculum and qualification reforms, so that young people can make the choices at 14 and at 16 about what and where to study which are right for them. This is particularly important as we introduce the new specialised Diplomas as new qualifications with the potential to engage more young people more fully in learning and tackle social and cultural stereotyping of the options available to them.

4.12 We are also reforming IAG for adults. We will complete by the end of the year a review of the wider potential for a comprehensive IAG service for adults. We launched in January this year a trial of an extended **learndirect** telephone service to provide a single point of access to in-depth personal guidance on learning, work and careers. We expect to help some 100,000 people during the trial period. We are working with SSCs to produce better labour market information to support this trial. Eventually there will be comprehensive information about all careers including pay rates and the economic value of particular qualifications which can be examined at local level. This will help to guide the career choices of people who are considering what new skills to develop, looking to re-enter the labour market, moving into a different industry or occupational area, or relocating to another part of the country.

4.13 At present there are estimated to be around 360,000 people on welfare benefits studying in FE. These are the people who most need help to raise their employment prospects through high quality, relevant programmes. Yet at present, no attention is paid to whether the programme they choose is relevant to their needs or would support a return to the labour market. We will work with DWP and Jobcentre Plus to ensure that welfare benefit recipients are encouraged to take up those learning opportunities that most directly improve their employability, including by referral to the LSC's local Nextstep face to face information and advice services and the national **learndirect** service.

Teaching and learning will be more tailored to individual needs

4.14 Every effective teacher, lecturer or trainer sets out as far as possible to meet the needs of all their students. In doing so, they can transform the life chances of learners. A range of practices to personalise learning, including the effective use of e-learning and new technology, aim to make the system as a whole more capable of responding to individual needs and aspirations. Effective use of data to track achievement, individual target setting and (especially for young people and learners with additional needs) linking together teaching and pastoral systems to identify problems and intervene fast can all help teachers to personalise learning.

4.15 At the heart of personalisation is that learners should have a proper assessment of their needs at the start of their programme – especially those without a Level 2 qualification. A learning plan should be drawn up to reflect the needs identified in the assessment, and reviewed regularly. This plan will shape the teaching and support delivered, as well as informing decisions to bring in help from other agencies. For learners aged up to 19, this information may already be available through the Common Assessment Framework, which should be built on and augmented rather than duplicated. The QIA will develop and disseminate resources based on existing effective practice models, to help providers ensure there is a robust assessment of need for all learners. LLUK will ensure that the ability to assess needs effectively is built into Initial Teacher Training.

4.16 Learners should also be supported to develop a range of effective learning styles in order to get the most from their programme and to take responsibility for managing their own learning. In short, we want all students in FE to become 'expert learners'. We know that knowing how to learn has a positive impact on retention, achievement and a learner's attitude to learning. The QIA, working with other agencies across the schools and learning and skills sectors, will develop a definition of, and standards for, the expert learner. The QIA's teaching and learning programme will ensure that structured support from subject teachers and other learning support helps individuals progress towards expertise in their learning. We will work with LLUK to ensure that the new Initial Teacher Training standards equip teachers to develop expert learners.

There will be better support for learners with learning difficulties or disabilities

4.17 In his report, Sir Andrew Foster highlighted the needs of learners with learning difficulties and/or disabilities (LLDD). He welcomed *Through Inclusion to Excellence* – the review, led by Peter Little, of provision for this group of learners – and the overarching recommendation that the LSC should develop a national strategy for the collaborative delivery of provision.

4.18 We are committed to higher standards for these learners. We are tackling concerns about the quality and consistency of LLDD provision, particularly within the network of independent specialist colleges catering for these learners. The establishment of the Foundation Learning Tier will help improve provision for this group. Key elements of implementing the report's recommendation will include:

- supporting collaborative working between agencies, to improve assessment of the needs of learners with learning difficulties and/or disabilities, and to improve the transition planning both into FE and training and into employment;

- an investment programme to develop high quality, innovative and collaborative provision;
- new LSC structures and responsibilities for LLDD, to ensure effective delivery of the strategy at local and regional level;
- ensuring that work related provision is accessible to learners with learning difficulties and/or disabilities; and
- a common funding approach, in line with the *agenda for change* proposals, which will enable better collaboration between providers.

There will be better pastoral support

4.19 Learners have a better chance of success where teaching and pastoral staff work closely together to focus on achievement. Often, those coming new to college or another large provider may find the choice and autonomy on offer challenging. Effective pastoral support is essential in these circumstances if learners are to settle and begin to achieve. So, the QIA will develop and issue guidance on effective pastoral support systems. Governing bodies should consider how their pastoral arrangements can best reflect the characteristics of their student body, including faith, for example through multi-faith chaplaincy arrangements.

4.20 In relation to young people, there is a particularly important challenge at key points of transition – often the move at age 16 from school to further learning. As part of our work to implement improved achievement at age 19 and reduce the proportion of young people not in employment, education and training, we will trial models of support which run across the age 16 boundary – so that learning support can be continuous and seamless across different institutions. We will trial this model initially in the 'hotspot' areas that face particular challenges in raising achievement at age 19.

We will support workforce development

4.21 The Foster report noted the need for a major enhancement of leadership and workforce development, and we strongly agree with this. Support for teachers and trainers to continue to develop and improve their practice is crucial to ensuring learners receive effective teaching tailored to their needs. We want to create, within the framework of the Quality Improvement Strategy, a well qualified workforce and a sustainable culture of professionalism, and to enable staff to improve and update their skills continuously.

We will reform initial training

4.22 We announced our plans to reform initial training for teachers, tutors and trainers in the sector in November 2004[3] and are taking these forward with LLUK. They include an 'Initial Award' (or 'Passport to Teaching'), Qualified Teacher Learning and Skills status, and the establishment of Centres for Excellence in Teacher Training, which will boost the professionalism of the sector's workforce.

4.23 In February 2006 Ofsted reviewed progress in initial teacher training and concluded that weaknesses remain. We agree with Ofsted that improvement is necessary, and believe that the reforms which will take effect from September 2007 will achieve that. With the support of initial teacher training providers, we have been piloting aspects of the reforms, including a core module in the effective use of technology and e-learning, and will publish the results in the autumn. We will ensure that the design of initial training programmes reflects the mission and purpose set out in Chapter 2, and that the new Centres for Excellence in Teacher Training recognise and promote excellence in vocational teaching.

4.24 We want all Skills for Life teachers to have easy access to high quality initial training, including part time programmes with integral teaching placements and mentoring support. We will fund accelerated intensive training routes through summer schools for returning teachers, teachers wanting to move into Skills for Life, and vocational teachers. This will support our objective of improving the quality of Skills for Life ESOL programmes.

We will improve professional development and introduce a new CPD requirement

4.25 Initial teacher training needs to be reinforced by continuing professional development. The best colleges and providers already prioritise the development of their workforce, but we must ensure the same happens everywhere and establish a more effective national structure to support that.

4.26 In September 2007 we will introduce a regulatory CPD requirement, applying to FE colleges, supported by a national CPD framework and guidance. We will consult on the arrangements for its introduction, including how to address national priority areas such as science and the early specialised Diploma lines, based on our intention to require:

- all teaching practitioners to fulfil, at the very least, 30 hours of CPD a year, with a reduced amount for part time teachers, and with similar expectations of managers and leaders;

3 DfES, *Equipping our Teachers for the Future*, November 2004.

- colleges and providers to draw up development plans for CPD, including in preparation for the introduction of the specialised diplomas and Train to Gain;
- teaching staff to maintain a portfolio of CPD that shows evidence of industrial/subject updating, including membership of appropriate professional bodies, development of skills in subject teaching, including the effective application of e-learning techniques, application of diversity and equal opportunity principles, and use of learner feedback to improve performance; and
- teaching practitioners to be professionally registered in order to maintain their licence to practise.

4.27 Within the CPD requirement, we propose a new framework for training the Skills for Life workforce, in the light of recent concerns over the quality of some programmes. This will draw together existing resources and training strategies into an integrated approach to drive up quality, differentiating between the training needs of the existing workforce and new recruits. We will establish a professional recognition scheme, to help experienced but under-qualified Skills for Life teachers and support workers to upgrade through a portfolio application process.

4.28 Strong management and leadership are crucial in all providers' drive to improve quality. We will introduce a qualification which all newly appointed college principals will be expected to achieve within a three year period. This will be developed in association with the CEL, and will recognize leadership expertise of those from other public sector or business backgrounds. The qualification will provide a nationally recognised standard against which governing bodies can assess potential candidates for positions as college principals. It will enhance the career development and job prospects of individuals. We will shortly consult on the arrangements for introducing this qualification.

We will improve recruitment and retention

4.29 The latest data[4] on staff recruitment and retention in the FE sector is generally encouraging:

- 82% of staff are very satisfied or fairly satisfied with their present jobs;
- turnover stands at 10%, comparing reasonably with other sectors, but it is higher in some vocational and subject areas; and
- 82% of respondents report engagement in some CPD.

4 DfES Research Report 697 'Recruitment and Retention in the Post-16 Learning and Skills Sector', York Consulting in association with MORI Social Research Institute (September 2004 - September 2005).

4.30 We already have in place a variety of recruitment incentives including Golden Hellos, training bursaries and the Key Worker Living scheme. We will introduce new programmes to increase recruitment, improve retention and promote diversity across the sector. We will invite LLUK to run these programmes, working with the CEL, trade unions and the employer bodies, and ensure that they link with similar schemes across the public and private sectors.

- The 'Give Something Back' programme, to be run in collaboration with the Skills for Business Network, will give technical and vocational specialists opportunities to teach in colleges and providers to fill key vacancies and to prepare the next generation for their industry. Initially, this will focus on supporting the new specialised Diplomas.
- The 'Make a Difference' programme will encourage high-flying graduates to make a career in the sector.
- 'Business Talent', a management recruitment programme as suggested by Sir Andrew Foster, will help colleges and providers attract exceptional talent from business and the public sector into senior management roles.
- 'Business Interchange' will offer teachers and trainers structured experience and training in relevant business sectors and create parallel opportunities for industry experts to give time to local colleges and providers.

4.31 As announced in the Budget on 22 March 2006, there will be an additional £11 million a year from 2007-08 for these new programmes.

4.32 Colleges and other providers need better intelligence on the current workforce and future needs. We will, through the work of LLUK, develop data collection arrangements for staffing across the sector in order to allow more accurate analysis and projections around supply and retention, while keeping the data collection burden to a minimum.

4.33 We are aware of the concern about pay differences between different types of provider. This is partly driven by the overall funding gaps between the schools and FE sectors, which we are committed to narrowing. We have already set out the steps we will take to narrow the gap from 13% to 8% by 2006-07, and beyond that we will take steps to narrow the gap further as resources allow. We believe it is important that colleges and providers retain the discretion to make their own decisions about pay for their staff, within their overall budget, rather than introducing national prescription. This will give them the flexibility to set pay to reflect their own priorities and mission, based on local labour market conditions.

We will promote greater equality and a more diverse workforce

4.34 Many colleges and providers make an exceptional contribution in promoting diversity and equality of opportunity for learners. However, Sir Andrew Foster rightly identified that there is more to be done to address the current lack of diversity within the workforce. Too many minority groups continue to be under-represented, especially at senior levels, and face barriers to progression in the sector.

- We will extend from 2006, eligibility for subsidies for services offered by the CEL, to include those currently under-represented in leadership positions. Through the CEL, we will offer coaching, mentoring and work-shadowing programmes tailored to the needs of under-represented groups.
- We will review the diversity of the workforce to ensure that the sector meets its legal obligations and actively promotes equality and diversity. That includes encouraging all providers and national agencies to adopt the Race Equality in Employment Standard, and developing an impact assessment approach to help providers test and strengthen their policies and procedures and broaden the diversity of the workforce.
- We will ask the CEL to introduce mandatory diversity competency modules to all their programmes, as part of their remit to transform the diversity of the sector. Diversity competence will become a requirement in the sector's professional qualifications. We will ask LLUK to assess annually the workforce diversity profile to ensure that all our actions are having a clear and demonstrable impact.

4.35 We are working with the LSC and other partners to ensure that colleges and other providers offer a safe learning environment, with proper safeguarding of young or vulnerable learners. We are undertaking a programme of work to ensure that robust arrangements are in place for vetting people who are in contact with young people and vulnerable adults. We will develop examples of good practice and expect all colleges and other providers to have clearly identified responsibilities for safeguarding arrangements within their governing bodies and management teams. We expect all those involved to be trained and supported in this role.

Chapter 5: A framework which spreads success and eliminates failure

We will support the development of the more personalised system we seek, by taking decisive action to eliminate failure and creating structures that help the best providers to spread their influence.

There is now much less failing and unsatisfactory provision in FE than in the recent past. We are now raising the bar to ensure that all provision is good or improving. Any provider or provision judged to be failing or coasting will be subject to an improvement notice. Colleges and other providers will receive support to address the problems immediately. If the problems are not addressed within a year, the LSC will be able to act decisively – changing governors, changing the leadership of the college, opening up the provision to competition or seeking a merger with, or help from, a strong provider.

At the same time, we will encourage new structural models, including federations, collaborative partnerships and trusts. These will all make it easier for the best providers to spread their influence across the system and to lead change. In addition, there will be a presumption that colleges meeting criteria to be designated 'high performing' will be able to expand their provision for 14-19 year-olds, particularly to provide new Diplomas. New competition arrangements will make it easier for new providers to enter the system, where significant expansion of high quality provision is needed. This will be underpinned by a new LSC remit to promote diversity, choice and specialisation.

A new balanced scorecard and overall performance rating (along the lines of the local authority Comprehensive Performance Assessment system) will provide greater transparency and public accountability for colleges.

5.1 Developing a new, more specialised system, focused on its core mission and the demands of learners and employers, and supporting ever more effective teaching and learning are crucial. We must also build an infrastructure which encourages the system as a whole to become more effective – tackling failure, encouraging innovation and spreading success. We want to ensure that we tackle failing or coasting provision swiftly and decisively and we must make it easier for the most effective providers to extend their reach more widely.

We will eliminate failure

5.2 We need to balance autonomy and reward for good colleges and other providers against robust intervention where standards are low. Outright failure in colleges is now very rare, although there is still too much poor provision in other training providers. And there is a much larger group of institutions (including, we estimate, up to 50 colleges or 12-15% of the total) which are barely satisfactory, or satisfactory but not improving, across much of their provision. Such colleges and other providers must improve rapidly. Our goal is to eliminate inadequate or unsatisfactory provision across the learning and skills sector by 2008 and to have a major impact on those organisations where performance is just satisfactory or not showing any improvement. These proposals for tackling failing and coasting provision mirror those set out in the recent *Higher Standards, Better Schools for All* White Paper.

5.3 There will be a robust intervention strategy to address inadequate, barely satisfactory and coasting (satisfactory, but not improving) colleges and provision, linked to the new funding method and new arrangements for college trusts, federations and mergers. Cases requiring intervention will be identified through inspection, other existing evidence, and new performance indicators described below. The precise nature of intervention will vary according to the circumstances: whether it involves the whole college or provider or just one area or department, and whether it is failing outright or coasting.

5.4 In all cases the LSC will issue a formal notice with a specified short period in which to see improvement (in most cases, one year). In the case of a failing college or provider the LSC will be able to withhold some or all of the commissioned element of its funding, and in other cases the LSC will judge what part of this funding to withhold. The college or provider will be allocated an improvement adviser from a national network to be established by the QIA from April 2006. The adviser will be an accredited expert with senior management experience in the sector. The QIA will also establish, with the LSC and the CEL, a cadre of high quality senior managers who can reinforce an existing management team as it works through the improvement plan, or replace the management on a temporary or permanent basis.

5.5 If, at the end of the period, there is not sufficient improvement, the LSC will implement one of a set of intervention options. There are four key types of intervention: change of leadership; change of governance; opening provision up to competition; and help from, or merger with, a stronger provider. Where a college or provider is failing outright, the strongest measures will apply. The LSC may hold a competition to find an alternative provider to take over responsibility from the existing provider, replace the governors or secure a merger with a highly-performing college.

5.6 Likewise, where an area or department of a college or provider is failing, the LSC will either hold a competition to replace failing provision, strengthen the governing body or require it to consider establishing a Trust, or direct the corporation to join a strong local federation, where one exists. Coasting colleges and provision will trigger similarly robust but less severe intervention measures.

5.7 This constitutes an important development of the LSC's role (which is changing, and is described more fully in Chapter 7). It will act as commissioner, with a more streamlined relationship with most colleges, but intervening robustly where necessary on behalf of the customer to ensure high quality across the board. Some of these intervention powers, including the power for the LSC to direct a governing body to dismiss a weak principal, will require new legislation, so we will look for a suitable opportunity to introduce this. For the time being, the Secretary of State's existing statutory powers, including change of governance, will be used. Through the new legislation we will also transfer these powers to the LSC.

5.8 This approach will be reinforced locally and regionally by the use of the new performance indicators and overall performance ratings described below and nationally by the DfES's performance management of the LSC and other organisations.

We will improve inspection

5.9 Inspection has contributed to recent improvements in quality. But inspection itself also has to keep adapting and improving as needs change.

There will be a new, integrated Ofsted and lighter touch inspection of the most successful institutions

5.10 Colleges will no longer need to engage with two separate inspectorates for FE. The changes to inspection services announced by the Secretary of State for Education and Skills in December 2005 will lead, subject to the necessary legislation, to a single inspectorate – the Office for Standards in Education, Children's Services and Skills in April 2007.

5.11 As is the case with schools, inspection of colleges and other providers will become much more selective, focusing on areas of weakness. New 'lighter touch' arrangements began in the second cycle of inspections in 2005, aiming to reduce the burden on colleges and providers. As a result, the average number of inspection days for colleges and other providers will reduce by 30%. Good and outstanding colleges and providers will see a reduction of around 50% and in some cases more. Also, as set out in Budget 2006, we will continue to work with public service inspectorates on further inspection reform and to assess the scope for reducing inspectorate expenditure by around a third over the medium term.

There will be better links with the QAA

5.12 HE programmes offered in colleges are subject to a different review regime, managed by the Quality Assurance Agency (QAA) on behalf of the HEFCE. The QAA will be consulting in late spring on proposals for a revised system from 2007/08 onwards, underpinned by the principles outlined above. We will ensure that the QAA and Ofsted, as a minimum, co-ordinate their activities so that they draw on the same data and self-evaluations. We will seek opportunities for further collaboration and alignment of approaches in the future and will ask Ofsted and the QAA to develop and test appropriate models.

There will be clearer information on performance

5.13 Clearer performance information will assist providers in their own quality assurance activities, facilitate the new selective approach to inspection and intervention, and help to assess value for money. The extensive information already available to learners and employers needs to be clearer and more accessible. The primary performance indicators need to be aligned with our reforms and allow straightforward and meaningful comparisons. At the same time, we need to reduce significantly the bureaucracy involved in the current arrangements across partner organisations for data collection, analysis, publication and use.

5.14 The new approach will build on the data and excellence themes of the LSC's *agenda for change* and the existing work on success measures. We will introduce a single, standard set of key indicators covering the broad themes of responsiveness, quality and resources.

Proposed Key Performance Indicators for Further Education and Skills

A. Responsiveness

1. Delivery against plan
2. Providers' responsiveness to employers (including employer satisfaction)
3. Providers' responsiveness to learners (including learner views/satisfaction and learner progression/destinations)

B. Quality

1. Learner (qualification) success rates
2. Quality of provision (via provider self-assessment validated by inspection and annual assessment visits)

C. Finance

1. Financial health
2. Financial control

5.15 The high level indicators summarise a number of measures demonstrating quality, responsiveness and financial performance. These dimensions have been chosen as they address how economically, efficiently and effectively resources have been used to meet the needs of individuals, employers and the wider community. When taken together the three dimensions provide an overall assessment of performance and value for money.

5.16 This approach will produce a balanced scorecard leading to a single, overall performance rating for each institution. The rating will categorise each institution on a scale ranging from excellent to poor. Building on approaches such as that adopted for local government, we will develop the scorecard and rating system in collaboration with providers and the LSC so that it gives a balanced assessment which providers themselves find useful.

5.17 The new indicators will also help inform choices for both learners and employers. They will feed into the Employer Guide to Training which we are developing and will contribute to information on 14-19 provision in each locality. They will also provide a useful evidence base for providers' own evaluation and improvement activities, help the QIA provide effective support, and be used by the LSC to inform judgements about funding and planning. A poor score in one or more of the indicators, will trigger the improvement actions described above. Excellent scores will lead to greater autonomy, in terms of streamlined planning and performance management and lighter inspection.

5.18 The indicators will draw on information from various sources, including the provider's own self-assessment, management information, survey data, inspection and audit, and possibly peer assessment. This should not increase bureaucracy, because much of the information is available from existing sources, and having one standard set of indicators used for multiple purposes will identify duplicate or surplus data. However, some of the indicators, such as information on learner destinations, will require additional effort and so we will consider very carefully the costs and benefits of each element of these proposals.

5.19 The LSC will consult on the approach and definitions in the early summer. We expect to establish prototype arrangements in 2007.

We will encourage innovation and new models of delivery

5.20 As the system develops, we want effective, confident colleges and other providers to have the freedom to develop and to innovate. Highly effective providers will increasingly have scope to spread their excellent practice more widely, especially through formal and informal collaboration.

Federations can improve quality

5.21 Federations can provide a powerful mechanism for quality improvement, with one strong college taking the lead in working with one or more others to share expertise and drive up standards. Federations involve the creation of formal, shared arrangements between two or more colleges within their governance structures – such as joint committees responsible for particular aspects of the two colleges' business. Over time, that may lead to merger, but there is no presumption that it must. In the new, more specialised system we are developing, federation can be particularly powerful in bringing together colleges with complementary strengths to improve opportunity for learners in both institutions. Over the next year, we will work with colleges and providers to invite proposals for pathfinder projects and to support them to be developed and implemented.

We will support new collaborative partnerships to promote delivery

5.22 We also want to encourage a wider range of collaborative models involving schools, colleges and other providers. These can have a range of purposes. For the 14-19 reforms in particular, collaboration between schools and colleges will be essential. Such collaboration could take a range of forms.

5.23 The current Education and Inspections Bill includes a formal power for maintained schools and colleges to collaborate. It enables the governing bodies of an FE college and one or more schools to collaborate formally as equal partners through joint committees with decision-making powers. Such arrangements can be used, for example, to manage the development and delivery of joint projects or to manage arrangements for school pupils to attend courses at a local college.

5.24 Similar formal collaborations (or more informal approaches) could also be used to develop and share expertise. For example, they might facilitate the development of the specialist networks described in Chapter 2. Collaborations to support joint professional development among staff – for example where they are delivering specialised Diplomas across more than one institution – could also be extremely powerful.

5.25 Collaborating to share services such as finance, personnel, procurement and estate management between providers can improve efficiency and release money for teaching and learning. The Foster report noted that administrative services could be rationalised to reduce duplication and waste. The LSC will lead the development of a shared services strategy, and will consider the need for financial incentives to establish provider networks.

Trusts can enable closer working with key partners

5.26 Some colleges may wish to form Trusts (not-for-profit charities) with other organisations, including businesses, schools, community groups and universities. A college with a strong identity as a specialist institution might form a Trust as a means of strengthening its relationship with one or more employers, perhaps as a means of ensuring that the employer voice is heard clearly as the college plans its provision and continues to move with the changing demands of the workplace. Where a college is already working in partnership with, for example, a local business, establishing a Trust could help formalise the arrangement and create a more sustainable structure for collaborative working.

5.27 It is also possible for groups of colleges to acquire a trust, and schools could be included in this. Such a Trust could be another way of bringing together a key group of local partners to deliver the 14-19 entitlement and ensuring that all of them are fully involved in developing courses that best meet the needs of young people. Acquiring a Trust is voluntary and will not change the legal status of a college. But the college may want to invite the Trust to appoint governors to the college's governing body and so strengthen that relationship further. Business and universities may also wish to consider forming Trusts to support one or more colleges, or involving colleges in Trusts they are setting up with schools. The Government and the LSC will work with colleges interested in setting up a Trust.

There will be a new 'Power to Innovate'

5.28 We also want colleges to exercise more actively the freedom and flexibility to try out new approaches, particularly in partnership with others. The Education and Inspections Bill includes a further new power: the 'Power to Innovate', which develops the powers introduced for schools in the 2002 Education Act. FE colleges already have very wide discretion to manage their own affairs. But the Power to Innovate will mean that if there are aspects of current education law which are getting in the way of valuable innovation which could improve provision for learners, colleges will be able to apply to the Secretary of State to grant exemptions or modifications to the law, for a time-limited period, to allow them to pilot a specific innovative proposal.

We will encourage new providers

5.29 In his review Sir Andrew Foster underlined the need to encourage new providers to enter the sector, and to enable high performing providers to expand. In particular, he recommended that greater use be made of tenders and competitions to reach out to potential new providers. We are putting in place a range of important measures to this end, in relation both to 16-19 year-olds and adults.

We will encourage new 16-19 provision through expansion opportunities and through competitions

5.30 In the next three years, we will need an additional 50,000 places for 16-19 year-olds, in order to meet growth in the size of the cohort and improvements in staying on rates. By 2015, we intend to have achieved 90% participation among 17 year-olds, compared to 75% now. Such growth in participation rates will be offset by a cohort which declines in size. Although no more additional places will be needed after 2007 an increasing proportion of those participating will be doing the new Diploma qualifications.

5.31 We have taken a number of steps to meet this demand for new places and to attract effective new providers into the system. We have established a new 'sixth form presumption' which means that there will be a presumption that high performing 11-16 specialist schools with a vocational specialism wishing to establish a sixth form should be allowed to do so, where they have space or resources to do so. This is backed with capital resources sufficient to allow the construction of up to 60 new sixth forms under the presumption.

5.32 Additionally, we have established a process for running competitions for 16-19 provision where there is a need for 200 or more new places in a local area on the grounds of capacity, quality or the need to extend diversity and choice. The LSC will decide whether there is such a need, given its duty to secure sufficient provision for delivery of the new 14-19 entitlement and the willingness of existing providers to offer suitable courses. These competitions will provide an important mechanism for high quality providers to expand and will be the key entry point into the publicly funded system for new providers. In deciding whether to hold a competition and in specifying what numbers of places and types of courses should be offered, the LSC will have regard to the overall strategic plan for the delivery of the new entitlement in the area, drawn up with the local authority as the strategic leader of services for children and young people. Once part of the publicly funded system, new providers will be expected to collaborate with other providers to deliver curriculum choice for 14-19 year-olds.

5.33 These measures will expand high quality provision, particularly to meet demand from 14-19 year-olds for the new specialised Diplomas. We want to ensure that the most effective colleges are able to expand provision to deliver Diplomas on the same basis as the most effective schools. Therefore, matching the sixth form presumption, we will introduce a corresponding presumption that high performing FE colleges and Sixth Form Colleges will be able to expand their provision for 16-19 year-olds in order to deliver specialised Diplomas. As with the sixth form presumption, the threshold for designation as 'high performing' will be deliberately high. This presumption will be backed by appropriate capital funding to build the required capacity.

We will give the LSC a new remit to encourage choice, diversity and specialisation and will introduce competitions to increase high quality provision

5.34 These measures are focused on 16-19 education. We want a more active approach to encouraging the entry of new providers across the whole sector. Within the Train to Gain programme, brokers will be able to bring in new providers to meet employer needs provided they meet required quality standards. And two further changes will be introduced. First, the LSC will be given a formal remit, through guidance from the Secretary of State, to secure choice, and diversity and specialisation of provision for learners and employers. Second, the principle of competitions and giving greater scope for high performing providers to expand will be extended beyond 16-19 education, in three ways:

- From 2007-08 the LSC will revise its approach to contracting for work based learning so that it is based on open competition. This will involve the awarding of approved supplier status to providers based on their performance in terms of the achievement rates of trainees. The numbers of training places which approved training providers are contracted to provide will be determined by local employer demand.

- Where institutions are providing poor quality, competitions will be held as a way of bringing in new providers to take over the service and raise quality. By 2008, the LSC will have stopped commissioning inadequate provision, and the proportion of barely satisfactory and coasting provision will have dramatically reduced.
- Some local pilots will be held in 2007-08 to test out extending formal competitions. This would involve putting out to competition substantial discrete blocks of provision, particularly where we need to expand participation. If these pilots are successful, the process will be extended across the country.

5.35 This will not be competition for its own sake. As part of its core commissioning role, the LSC will review provision in each area every 5 years and establish whether a competition is needed to improve quality, promote innovation, or expand provision. Existing providers from around the country will be able to bid, as well as new providers. All providers will be required to meet rigorous quality criteria set by the LSC in consultation with Ofsted and the QIA, including their ability and commitment to collaborate with other providers where appropriate to deliver curriculum choice in 14-19 learning. New providers will be eligible for additional funding support for a limited period where that is required to build their capacity.

Chapter 6: Funding which supports our objectives

We need a funding system which supports the FE system to move in the direction outlined in this White Paper. Funding will be targeted on priority areas and follow the needs of learners and employers – with young people's choices funded in full and increasing amounts of funding for adult learning flowing through demand-led mechanisms – Learner Accounts and Train to Gain.

The new entitlement to free tuition for all 19-25 year-olds studying for their first full Level 3 qualification will be funded in full, while for other provision, we will move towards a fee contribution of around 50%for adults who are not entitled to free tuition. We will continue to support low-income learners to ensure that they are not prevented from participating in priority programmes and will extend the Adult Learning Grant to full national coverage from September 2007, to help meet the additional costs of learning.

These proposals will be backed through regional and local plans to improve the quality and diversity of provision, determining the pattern of new capital investment. Local authorities will be asked to expand the scope of Building Schools for the Future (BSF) visions to include FE provision for 14-19 year olds, so that they are fully comprehensive in setting out what will be required in a locality to deliver our 14-19 reform programme. LSC capital will be directed to implementing this vision, alongside BSF resources.

6.1 Our plans for focusing the system more fully on a core employability mission rely on creating a funding system which rewards that focus. Similarly, funding must better follow the needs and choices of learners and employers if the system as a whole is to respond to them. And funding should reward good quality provision, enable the removal of unsatisfactory provision and encourage new providers. Funding reform is therefore a key enabler.

6.2 We will develop and implement a new approach to funding for 14-19 year-olds enabling the delivery of a curriculum entitlement to an individual through more than one provider. We will ensure that funding for adult learning is demand-led and focus funding on the priorities, with targeted support for disadvantaged adult learners. Capital investment will support specialisation and ensure that provision for 14-19 year-olds is driven by the choices of students and parents.

We will introduce a new approach to funding for 14-19 year-olds

6.3 Our aim in reforming education and training for 14-19 year-olds is to create a system where more young people are prepared by their education for success in life. Teenagers need a broad education which equips them not just for progression in learning and a particular job today, but gives them the right foundations for their adult lives – as individuals, in the family and in the community as well as at work.

We will implement a new set of principles for 14-19 funding

6.4 The principles which will inform the development of our approach to funding are:

- Funding methods and allocations must not drive young people's choices about the education and training route they follow. On the contrary, their choices – informed by high quality advice and guidance – must drive funding allocations so that they can pursue the programme best meeting their needs.
- Comparable funding must be allocated for comparable activity, irrespective of the type of institution that is providing the education and training.
- Where a programme is best delivered by attending more than one institution, the method must support that, with incentives for providers to collaborate in providing a high quality, coherent and seamless programme for the young person. It must avoid creating incentives for institutions to seek to persuade students to spend either more, or less, of their time on programmes delivered within that institution than is in the best interest of that student.
- The funding method must recognise the genuine additional costs of learners studying and training in more than one institution. Each local 14-19 partnership should be supported to meet such costs.
- The method should not fund the same learner twice to attend different institutions, and should incentivise institutions to pursue cost-effectiveness, including through specialisation.

- Funding should support and incentivise institutions to improve participation, progression and achievement rates. This should apply not just for those students who remain in their own institution, but to all young people in that local area.
- Schools and colleges must have discretion as to how to spend their budgets.
- Funding should be through a single system as far as possible, rather than through separate ring-fenced budgets.
- The method must be transparent, simple for institutions to understand and operate, provide appropriate stability and certainty for future planning, and avoid unnecessary bureaucracy.

6.5 We will press ahead as rapidly as possible to test the practical implications and technical consequences of these principles. This will be done in consultation with schools, colleges, training providers, local authorities and the LSC and we will examine the detailed options through a technical funding group involving representatives of these groups. We are committed to ensuring that we avoid undue turbulence.

6.6 We are legislating to provide a new curriculum and qualifications entitlement for 14-19 year-olds, through the current Education and Inspection Bill. This will place new duties to secure sufficient provision to meet the entitlement, on local authorities in relation to 14-16 year-olds and on the LSC for 16-19 year-olds. Both the local authority and LSC have crucial roles in delivery and their funding powers will need to be used to enable them to play those roles effectively. We want local authorities to play the strategic leadership role, consistent with their leadership role in children's services overall, ensuring the integration of the delivery of 14-19 reform with the wider agenda for children and young people in the locality. Within that, the LSC remains the primary partner for the local authority, using its funding and powers to secure rapid and high quality implementation of the 16-19 entitlement in every area. In practice, we want to see local authorities and the LSC working together to drive progress through a shared strategy, as many are already doing. We will work through Government Offices and the LSC to ensure that there are arrangements in place in each area to monitor delivery of 14-19 reform and the new statutory entitlements in particular, and to intervene if necessary.

Funding will support delivery of the new 14-19 entitlement

6.7 By creating a new curriculum and qualifications entitlement for young people, we intend to make sure that more young people are able to pursue courses meeting their needs and qualifying them for success. The breadth of the new entitlement will mean that schools, colleges and other providers will need to work together to deliver it. Therefore many more young people will spend part of their time studying away from their home institution, in order to take advantage of facilities and teaching in a college or elsewhere. Significant numbers already do this, for example through the Increased Flexibility Programme. Mainstream funding must be designed to support this pattern of study.

6.8 This pattern of provision of the entitlement also means that there should be a single, integrated funding system for school sixth forms, colleges and training providers, based on the approach set out in the LSC's *agenda for change*. We are committed to establishing a common funding approach across school sixth forms, colleges and training providers in which comparable learning is funded at a comparable rate. We have already taken steps to narrow by around 5 percentage points the funding gap between school sixth forms and colleges, and by a further 3 percentage points from 2008. When resources allow, further steps will be taken.

6.9 We propose to examine whether funding for 14-16 learning should be distributed so that, where a young person attends more than one institution, each is funded for their share of a young person's learning programme, as happens for 16-19 year-olds now. This might reflect the proportion of time spent by the student at each institution, while recognising that the home institution will also have some additional costs. We will look at whether such a system should reflect different programme costs, balancing accuracy of cost calculation against simplicity of administration. And we will consider whether there is a compelling case for national prescription in these areas or whether local discretion is preferable.

6.10 There are several possible distribution models. For example, all the money could go to the home school, which would then pay the other school or college its share. In this system, schools could receive an additional weighting for those pupils studying off site, to reflect the additional costs of this form of provision. Alternatively, the system could be managed centrally, as some local authorities are doing with the additional resources allocated through the Dedicated Schools Grant for off-site vocational provision in Key Stage 4 in 2006-07 and 2007-08.

6.11 Additionally, we are currently supporting local capacity building and the costs of collaboration, transport and other costs of partnership through dedicated funding streams. In total, we will provide £22 million in 2006-07 and in 2007-08 for this. In the longer term, we will look at the potential for bringing these resources within mainstream funding.

6.12 As set out in the 14-19 Implementation Plan, we are establishing a set of pilots to test out different models for local planning and funding to deliver the 14-19 entitlement, which will inform developments over the long term as we work through to full implementation of the entitlement by 2013.

We will introduce progression measures

6.13 New performance indicators announced in the *14-19 Education and Skills* White Paper will incentivise providers to focus on the future achievement and progression of all young people. They will show what proportion of young people leaving a school go on to achieve Level 2 by the age of 19, and what proportion go on to achieve Level 3 by that age. We will consider drawing on those indicators as part of the funding system to strengthen the incentives for providers, individually and collectively, to encourage progression, not just for those students who stay in their institution but also for those who move to another provider or job with training.

We will ensure that more adult funding is demand-led

6.14 The principle of funding following learner choice must also apply for adults. The LSC's *agenda for change* funding system already reflects this principle strongly, in that funding allocations for colleges and training providers are based on student numbers. But we want progressively to move to a position where more funding is driven directly by employer and learner choice.

6.15 We will do this by increasing the proportion of the adult skills budget that is allocated according to the demands of its key customers. We have set out our plans to trial an accounts scheme for adult learners at Level 3, giving them direct control of the public funding allocated to support their learning. Similarly, we have set out plans to empower employers as customers of FE through the Train to Gain brokerage and funding system, including in purchasing HE level training. These programmes will strengthen the incentives for colleges and training providers to respond quickly and flexibly to learner and employer needs.

6.16 Furthermore, the 'commissioned' element of the funding system within *agenda for change* provides the leverage to respond to other forms of demand, less easily expressed through Train to Gain or Accounts. In particular, it provides the way to respond to the aggregate demand of employers, expressed through SSAs and the regional skills priorities set out in the Regional Economic Strategies. The LSC will review how the *agenda for change* funding system can incorporate the increasingly demand-led approach, so that funding for providers is directly driven by the decisions of employers and learners, without creating new bureaucracy through multiple payment systems.

6.17 Overall, through the different demand-side mechanisms and drawing on the experience of the funding trials, we estimate that the share of the adult training budget which is demand-led will grow to some 40% by 2010-11 from below 20% in 2006-07. We expect that this direction of travel will then continue, so that a majority of the funding is demand-led by 2015-16.

Funding will be targeted on our priorities

6.18 In support of the new mission of the FE system, we will ensure that our national funding priorities are clear. It is strongly in the collective national interest for all young people to gain a good foundation of education and training to prepare them for adult and working life. Therefore, public funds will continue to pay for all education and training for young people through to the age of 19, without charging any fees to students – and the new Level 3 entitlement for 19-25 year-olds will extend that principle. But for older adults the arguments are different. The state cannot and should not pay for all education and training for adults. Adults and their employers receive substantial direct benefits from many forms of training and qualifications, in the form of higher wages and higher productivity. It is only fair that they should contribute to the cost.

We will continue to fund our existing priorities

6.19 In the *21st Century Skills* White Paper of July 2003, we set out our priorities for public funding of adult learning. They remain:

- Skills for Life programmes, to enable adults to improve their basic skills of literacy and numeracy;
- first full Level 2 qualifications to enable adults to achieve the platform of skills they need for employment, progression and success in further learning and work;
- supporting the development of technician, advanced craft and associate professional skills (Level 3), particularly where those meet sectoral and regional skills priorities;
- supporting those who are re-skilling for new careers, and those preparing to return to the labour market, again particularly where that meets sectoral and regional skills priorities; and
- safeguarding a varied range of learning opportunities for personal fulfilment, community development and active citizenship.

6.20 Between 2003-04 and 2005-06, an extra £200 million was directed from other provision to these priorities. Many of these priorities will help adults disadvantaged in the labour market to get back into productive, sustainable work, particularly those who are receiving welfare benefits. At the same time, we have introduced higher fees, to raise a larger contribution from employers and learners for other types of programme, while retaining the national fee remission arrangements to make sure that the least well off are not excluded from learning.

6.21 In *Priorities for Success*, we said that our intention was that the national fee assumption should rise further over time to around 50%, while continuing to protect groups of priority learners through fee remission, and to invest public funds in the priority areas of learning. We are now confirming that the national fee assumption for adult learners will rise to around 50% in the 2010/11 academic year. In addition, we have signalled the intention to cease funding some types of provision which the public purse should not support: for example, health and safety qualifications for employees for which employers should cover the full cost, and very short courses normally taken by better qualified learners.

6.22 The FE sector will play a vital role in leading the rebalancing of public and private funding for education and training required to meet the skills challenges of the next decade. We accept that rebalancing funding in this way will be challenging, and as we have said before, colleges and providers will require support from the LSC in making this change.

We will fund the new entitlement for 19-25 year-olds

6.23 It is important that young adults are not penalised by the increase in fees to around 50% in relation to their counterparts studying in HE. So we are introducing the entitlement to full fee remission for a first full Level 3 qualification for the 19-25 age group. This will cover the equivalent of a two A level package, and will include Access to HE programmes. Young adults in this age group will therefore pay nothing for the opportunity to gain the qualifications generally required to progress to HE.

6.24 This new entitlement recognises that many young people are in effect continuing their initial education into their early twenties. In addition, 19-25 year-olds are more likely to want to study full time and less likely to have an independent full time source of income to cover the cost of fees. In 2004/05 there were 44,000 19-25 year-olds enrolled on full Level 3 courses in FE. In future they will be counted as a category of learner entitled to full remission of fees, on the same basis as adults studying for their first full Level 2 under the Level 2 entitlement. Advanced Apprenticeships will be included in the 19-25 entitlement as free to the young person. The employer will continue to contribute around 33% of the cost in line with current arrangements, reflecting the greater worth of an Apprenticeship in increasing productivity.

6.25 As we develop the Foundation Learning Tier (FLT) as a coherent framework of units and qualifications below Level 2 (as set out in Chapter 3), and as resources allow, we will extend the entitlement for 19-25 year-olds to those FLT programmes which most effectively support progression to Level 2 and beyond (the 'progression pathways').

6.26 In the trials of accounts, all our support for 19-25 year-old learners will be brought together through the account mechanism. In the pilot areas, both fee remission and the Adult Learning Grant will be paid through the account. In developing the new approach to support for 19-25 year-olds, DfES and DWP will work with other partners to improve access to learning for young, disadvantaged adults, helping them to overcome the barriers to remaining in or returning to learning.

We will implement our new principles for fees

6.27 Full fee remission for adults on income related welfare benefits will be focused increasingly on those taking a first full Level 2 (or a first full Level 3 if more appropriate), a Skills for Life course or a programme of learning within the FLT which supports progression. Entitlement to full fee remission will be time limited from the point when the individual begins learning and not open ended, in order to provide the greatest incentive for progression through to Level 2 and beyond.

6.28 By 2010, the assumed national fee contribution for learners not covered by the national entitlements will rise to around 50%, wherever they are following courses that lead to credit based units or qualifications within the Framework for Achievement and designated by the relevant SSC (or other recognised body) as valued by employers in promoting employability, or developing higher level vocational skills. Our approach will be guided by our wider strategy to raise the level of contributions from employers and learners who can afford to pay, in order to redirect funds to support growth in priority areas of learning.

6.29 The level of fees and subsidy for PCDL programmes will depend on local choice about how to use the allocated resources, except family learning which will remain free. All other adult learning, including company specific training and training which is used by employers to meet their statutory obligations (whether included in the Framework for Achievement or not) will have no public subsidy.

6.30 To support this general change in approach, the LSC has introduced a system of fee income targets in 2005-06. These are negotiated individually with each college and take into account their particular mix of learners and the mix of learning programmes they offer. They provide the essential basis for ensuring that fee income is raised rather than learning opportunities cut or simply under funded.

We will support learners financially

6.31 Alongside the fee regime focused on the direct costs of learning, we shall continue to offer financial support to help those individuals whose means and circumstances would otherwise make it impossible for them to participate. Education Maintenance Allowances are available to 16 year-olds (and to 17 year-olds from 2006-07) in all parts of the country to help young people from poorer families to stay on in full time education and training rather than feeling obliged to start earning a wage. They have had a positive impact on staying on rates.

Education Maintenance Allowance

As Jodie Farrington came to the end of year 11 she was all set to leave school behind to pursue a career in hairdressing. However, the introduction of the Education Maintenance Allowance (EMA) made Jodie reconsider. She stayed at school to undertake four A levels and has now set her sights on a degree in English or Business Studies.

Jodie comments, "Money was an issue when I was thinking about what to do after my GCSEs. Getting a job seemed like the best option, but then I found out about EMA and it made me realise that I could afford to stay on and do my A levels and buy the books and equipment I would need. When I got my GCSE results and saw they were good enough to go on and do A levels that confirmed my decision and I haven't looked back."

Jodie receives £20 per week EMA, which she spends on travel expenses, course books and lunch each day. The money means she doesn't have to undertake part time work, helping Jodie to focus her attention on achieving the best possible results. Her predicted grades have now significantly increased, leading Jodie to contemplate university. She says, "I know I didn't work as hard as I could have during my GCSEs, but that has all changed – partly because I now get £100 EMA bonus payments for good attendance and coursework. It has been a big motivation for me and has encouraged me to put more effort in. I am really pleased with the improvement in my grades and want to carry on doing my best – not just for the money but also for my own personal satisfaction."

6.32 For adult learners in FE, by 2007-08 the LSC will be providing £145 million of financial support including an additional £11 million allocated in Budget 2006. The main component is the Learner Support Funds which are disbursed at the discretion of colleges. They are targeted at learners who would otherwise face financial difficulties in starting or completing courses, and will continue to offer a safety net to the most disadvantaged learners.

6.33 The LSC is also currently carrying out regional trials of a means tested Adult Learning Grant. This typically provides up to £30 per week for disadvantaged adult learners undertaking full time courses in FE. Evidence so far shows that the grant is particularly valuable for young people in their early twenties studying for their first Level 3 qualifications, in many cases working part time and living with their parents. The grant will therefore form a valuable complement to the 19-25 entitlement. The additional £11 million allocated in Budget 2006 will bring forward the roll out of the Adult Learning Grant to achieve national coverage by 2007-08.

6.34 This package of financial support, coupled with the entitlements to free and subsidised tuition costs set out earlier, will support effectively the most disadvantaged learners. Over the period 2007-08 to 2010, fee contributions for learning outside the main priority groups will increase further as set out above. As these changes are introduced, and in light of the new 19-25 entitlement, we will review the package of learner support funds to ensure they continue to meet the needs of adult learners and are most effectively targeted to provide appropriate incentives for individuals seeking to invest in improving their skills. We shall continue to ensure a high priority is given to programmes that improve the employment chances of people at a disadvantage in the labour market.

We will invest in facilities to deliver

6.35 The Foster review recognised that the current condition of premises and equipment affects the reputation of the sector, with too many learners still studying in poor surroundings. Capital investment must improve facilities and the wider environment, but also has a crucial role in implementing our priorities for young people and adults, particularly through supporting specialisation, widening choice and improving access.

6.36 In future, national and regional capital strategies will be developed by a group of partners led by the LSC and including Regional Skills Partnerships, to guide investment to meet the priorities set out in this White Paper. This will ensure that there is sufficient capacity, an effective pattern of specialisation and increasing choice, access and responsiveness for learners and employers.

6.37 At the same time, we want to remove some of the inconsistencies between the school and college capital regimes which may distort delivery of the 14-19 programmes. We also want to address the difficulty work based learning and new providers have in securing capital funding to develop their capacity, as part of the commitment to fair contestability.

6.38 In line with the strategic leadership role of local authorities in delivering 14-19 reform, we will ask them to extend the scope of their BSF visions to cover all the settings in which young people aged 14-19 will be learning in the future. This will mean that the BSF visions will become fully comprehensive in setting out the facilities that will be required in a locality in order to deliver the new 14-19 reforms. The additional capital resources allocated in Budget 2006 for 11-19 year-olds will become an important part of delivering the full local BSF visions.

6.39 The LSC will be fully involved in developing and drawing up the local vision as it affects the FE sector and will ensure that it is consistent with the regional capital strategy. The LSC will also continue to take an overview of the college's or provider's whole capital strategy and needs. But wherever the costs of capital development exceed the resources available through BSF to enable colleges and providers to contribute to the 14-19 entitlement, the LSC's capital funding must be directed to implement in full the FE component of the 14-19 capital vision as it is developed in each locality. This will mean that for the first time, there is effectively a fully integrated capital strategy which will deliver for 14-19 year-olds across schools and the FE system.

6.40 The LSC's capital programme will therefore:

- Ensure that regional capital strategies reflect regional and local plans to improve choice, quality and diversity. Those strategies must in turn drive the approval criteria for individual capital proposals.
- Support the expansion and reorganisation of provision in local areas to secure the capacity for high quality specialised Diploma programmes and the entitlement. To ensure the right organisational solution in each local area and to remove barriers to participation in competitions, we will be prepared to pay up to 100% grant funding for 14-19 capital projects in the FE sector. To ensure value for money, each institution's financial circumstances will still be taken into account, but we do not want differential levels of capital support to distort the pattern of provision.
- Prioritise the capital support necessary to enable high performing FE and Sixth Form Colleges to expand their vocational provision for 16-19 year-olds as part of the 'FE presumption'.
- Extend eligibility to capital grant to new providers and training providers where necessary to secure substantial, new high quality provision as part of a long term commitment to supply.
- Allocate capital to support the policy of specialisation, particularly to develop National Skills Academies, CoVEs and sectoral networks. There will be new grants for specialist equipment to help refocus mission and accelerate the rate of specialisation across the sector.

6.41 The capital investment outlined here will contribute to the LSC's sustainable development strategy *From Here to Sustainability*, published in September 2005. This set the vision for a learning and skills sector that will contribute to sustainable development through its management of resources, the effective application of new technologies, the learning opportunities it delivers and its engagement with communities. The LSC will publish a full prospectus on the capital programme in the autumn.

Chapter 7: A new relationship with colleges and providers

The changing nature of society and the economy place major demands on colleges and providers to prepare young people better for life and work and to improve the skill levels of the workforce. If the FE system is to meet these demands, then we need a new relationship with colleges and providers, which will release more of providers' energy to focus on improvement and meeting the needs of learners.

We will implement a simplified system for planning and funding provision, which will make clearer the links between national priorities and local action, and enable colleges to play more fully to their strengths. A single named strategic partner will lead for the LSC in its relationship with each college or provider. There will be improved communications between government and its agencies and the system: there will be a single gateway process for all publications and data returns, which will ensure that only relevant, clear and important communications are sent as a matter of course to providers. Improved arrangements for data collection will ensure that data is collected once and used many times. There will be new freedoms from the planning infrastructure for the most effective providers.

The system as a whole will align itself behind the efforts of colleges and providers. Both the DfES and the LSC are implementing radical reductions in staffing levels and introducing different ways of working. In becoming a more strategic Department, the DfES is stopping a number of activities and moving operational activities to the LSC. The LSC is becoming a 'strategic commissioner', strengthening both its ability to plan at regional level and its ability to work at the level of local authorities, while reducing staffing. The system as a whole will be underpinned by a national learning model, designed to ensure that resources are deployed to maximum effect for the economy and for society.

7.1 If the FE system is to be capable of responding to the challenges of 14-19 reform and improving adult skills as this White Paper proposes, then we need to reshape the relationship between central government (and its agents) and education and training providers to release more of their energy, initiative and dynamism. We want to develop a new relationship with colleges and other providers which removes unnecessary bureaucracy, secures better alignment between local and national objectives, supports individual institutions to improve and build capacity (including through strong networks) and holds providers to account in ways which are rigorous, but lighter touch and proportional.

7.2 As we continue to develop this new relationship, we will also be ensuring that key national institutions are aligned behind it. We will clarify and simplify roles and responsibilities and slim down the key national organisations.

The new relationship will aim to cut burdens and develop a self-improving system

7.3 Our aim is a system where colleges and other providers are able to focus fully on their own improvement and on delivering ever more effectively to learners, rather than on unnecessarily complex requirements from other organisations. We will continue to reform the external planning, accountability and support systems, so that the burden they impose decreases and so that providers find these systems coherent and effective in supporting them to make the improvements they seek.

The system for agreeing plans and funding will be simplified

7.4 At the heart of the new relationship will be simpler processes for agreeing what each provider will receive public funds to do. These processes are intended to develop stronger relationships of trust between the LSC and providers, to establish a clearer line of sight between national and local priorities and targets, and to allow the level of external intervention in a provider's planning to vary according to its effectiveness.

7.5 Each year, after analysing local, regional and sectoral performance and demand, the LSC will identify a small number of priorities which will inform local and regional plans for government-subsidised provision. Colleges and other providers will propose what they should contribute based on their knowledge of local needs. The annual planning dialogue between providers and the LSC will then focus on agreeing priorities and funds within plans and then reviewing performance and delivery against those plans.

7.6 The planning dialogue will be founded on each provider's own processes for planning, evaluation and improvement, including self-assessment. The LSC has set out in *agenda for change* and *Planning for Success* how it will move to such a simple and transparent planning framework from 2006-07. 2006 will be a transitional year, with further changes being implemented in full in 2007.

There will be a single LSC strategic partner

7.7 Within this planning framework, there will in future be a single nominated LSC strategic partner for each college or other provider, who will co-ordinate the relationship and all discussions for the LSC. They will be responsible for discussing priorities, negotiating plans and commissioning provision on the basis of needs and priorities, focusing particularly on mission, specialisation, collaboration, and performance.

7.8 For most colleges and providers, conversations will take place twice a year, once to agree a plan and once to review performance against it. Otherwise, dialogue will only occur where there are issues of concern, or mutual benefit, or where the provider itself initiates the contact. The LSC will of course intervene as often as necessary where there is underperformance.

7.9 The skills of the LSC strategic partner will be key, to develop a partnership which adds real value for the college or provider. As part of its work to develop the structures, staffing and competence to deliver its *agenda for change* reforms, the LSC is working with the sector to define the skills and experience required for such a role.

7.10 We want to create a modern, more self regulating form of college autonomy where colleges work together to set, review and raise standards and achieve continuous improvement in the interests of learners, employers and the local community. We will work with colleges, the AoC and other representative organisations to develop proposals for greater self regulation which make a reality of this vision.

We will improve communications with colleges and other providers

7.11 We expect the new approach to have significant benefits in improving the coherence and clarity of communication and in improving the flow of information in both directions. In addition, in response to continuing concerns about the number of documents and requests for information, the LSC will introduce a single gateway for all its publications and data returns. This will be modelled on the gateway for publications sent to schools. No publications or returns will be issued without first being checked with a panel of practitioners, drawn from the sector, for clarity, relevance and ease of implementation. The DfES will not in future routinely send publications or returns to colleges and providers. Any publications or return requests that are issued will go through the gateway process. The LSC will work with the sector to determine the best way to operate the gateway and to allow for legitimate information requests that cannot be anticipated, such as Freedom of Information requests.

7.12 Similarly, the QIA and other key partners are working together to improve the coherence of quality improvement information. The QIA will hold all its material and resources on its website and distribute a regular newsletter to ensure that providers are kept informed. However, good practice and research publications will be distributed only to those who order them. The QIA will work with a panel of practitioners to set guidelines for, and keep under review, the scope and usefulness of the materials it sends out or places on its website.

The burden of the examination system will be reduced

7.13 Rationalising qualifications through Diplomas and the Framework for Achievement will make a major contribution to reducing bureaucracy for colleges and other providers. But action is needed more broadly to tackle the administrative burdens created by the current qualifications system. The QCA is working with awarding bodies and others to rationalise requirements. By 2008, a web-based system will be introduced to streamline examination administration for general qualifications and specialised Diplomas.

7.14 Reducing the overall burden of bureaucracy is a key objective. We want to ensure that the monitoring of colleges by awarding bodies and other organisations relates directly to risk. Colleges with a good record of qualifications delivery should have fewer checks than those where there are quality concerns. In addition, the burden of multiple awarding body inspections must be reduced. The QCA will work with the LSC, the inspectorates, sector representatives and awarding bodies to identify the basis on which robust judgements can be made. A new approach will be trialled by the start of the 2007/08 academic year and introduced more widely in 2008/09.

7.15 The financial burden of the examinations system must also be addressed. Current administrative arrangements are expensive for colleges and other providers. The DfES, LSC and AoC are developing new ICT based systems so that colleges and providers can work together and access new collaborative procurement arrangements for goods and services, including assessment services.

7.16 In addition, we must ensure that the fees charged by awarding bodies to colleges are reasonable. The key is to establish an effective, competitive market and transparency of fees from different awarding bodies on a comparable basis. At present, it is difficult for colleges to compare costs for comparable qualifications across awarding bodies because there is no common format for the presentation of fees. The QCA will lead a review of fees, working with other interested organisations, including those representing the schools sector. The review will consider both the level of fees and how, in partnership with the awarding bodies, a common format might be created for implementation by the start of the 2007/08 academic year. The review will start by considering fees for GCSEs and A levels, and progress to look at other widely used qualifications. Their initial report is scheduled for publication this Autumn.

Data systems will be reformed to cut the burden of collection and to ensure that providers have the most useful information about learners

7.17 Good information is fundamental for colleges and other providers working to improve their performance. It is equally central to target setting and performance management and to achieving a streamlined, non-bureaucratic set of relationships for planning, funding and management.

7.18 The LSC is making good progress towards improving both the collection and use of information through the MIAP (Managing Information Across Partners) programme and *agenda for change*. For example, the project is developing a learning data interface, which will enable learners (and with their consent, learning providers) to access individualised learner records, using a unique learner number. These records will bring together information currently collected from schools, FE, HE, and awarding bodies. There have also been significant improvements arising from the work of the Bureaucracy Review Group.

7.19 To build on this, we intend to bring together the information needs of all the organisations who request information from the sector and agree what will be required from all providers, based on common standards. This will mean that data is collected once and used for a variety of purposes. We will ensure that only priority information is collected and that reports are made back in a standard format.

7.20 We will do so by establishing a single mechanism or gatekeeper for setting information standards and data and reporting requirements. We will set up an operational body or data agency to implement these requirements. As suggested by Sir Andrew Foster, we are exploring options including giving the Higher Education Statistics Agency (HESA) new responsibilities for post-16 data or simplifying the current LSC arrangements through a strong annual information agreement between colleges or providers and key data users.

There will be new freedoms for high performing providers

7.21 This new system is being developed to be proportionate, so that high performing providers are not subject to unnecessary scrutiny, and intervention is in inverse proportion to success. In addition, we have set out in previous chapters our plans to harness the talents of successful leaders to play a wider role in reform. This could be through merger or federation or through increasing volumes of provision through the 'commissioned' element of the new funding system or it could be through taking on the role of 'improvement partner' to support the improvement of a provider where there is weakness.

7.22 We want to explore further options for freeing the excellent. We will look at the scope for introducing 3 year funding agreements for the most effective providers; and at whether for these colleges 3 year (rather than annual) submission of business plans could be an improvement. If these measures were adopted, it would be possible to reduce further in most years the required level of dialogue with the LSC. It could also be possible to move to a single data return and student number projection in each year.

7.23 In support of these proposals, we will establish a Ministerial Standing Group on Further Education, chaired by the Minister of State for Lifelong Learning, Further and Higher Education and including the Chief Executives of the major agencies, key representative bodies and providers themselves. The group will review progress in implementing the vision set out in this White Paper. Its role will include ensuring that the proposals for streamlined ways of working outlined here are implemented effectively. It will consider in particular whether there is more to be done to free high performing providers, and will invite proposals from those providers as to the freedoms they would like to see.

We will streamline the system to support the new relationship

7.24 This new relationship will be supported by a more streamlined system. Within a robust accountability framework, we seek to make sure that the roles of all the key partners are clear, distinct and coherent in their support for the colleges and providers working to offer an excellent service.

DfES, LSC and other national partners will be slimmer and more focused

7.25 Sir Andrew Foster's report noted the widespread perception that the respective roles of the DfES and LSC are not clear, and that there is too much duplication. We agree that there is more to be done to clarify the roles and responsibilities and ensure that we eliminate the potential for overlap.

7.26 The role of the DfES is to provide strategic leadership, secure effective delivery of national targets and objectives, determine the policy framework and exercise the responsibilities of a Department of State. The LSC offers advice on strategy and policy and ensures that the system delivers services for learners and employers efficiently and effectively. To reinforce this distinction, the LSC has now taken responsibility for a number of areas of clearly operational work, including basic skills and offender learning. Subject to legislation, the LSC will also take powers to enable it to eradicate poor provision. The existing DfES/LSC concordat will be updated to reflect the new relationship and the behaviours and actions that underpin it.

7.27 We are ensuring that both organisations are fit for purpose. Sir Andrew Foster identified a significant concern that too many people, some with overlapping roles, were overseeing the sector. Both DfES and the LSC agree that they should reduce in size. Therefore, as part of the wider programme of Government efficiency savings, the DfES is reducing staff numbers by some 30% – including reducing by 325 the numbers in Lifelong Learning and Skills Directorate – and the LSC as part of *agenda for change* is reducing its numbers by 1,100. Both DfES and the LSC are introducing new organisational structures and ways of working. We will review the staff reductions and organisational structures set out here in 2008, in order to ensure that they reflect the roles set out above, and will continue to develop the efficiency and effectiveness of both organisations as necessary to support improvement in the system.

7.28 The LSC will have a leading role in delivering this White Paper. It has made good progress in recent years, with an impressive record of achieving its targets, for example on Apprenticeships and Skills for Life. This White Paper strongly reinforces the new direction set by *agenda for change*, so that the LSC works with providers and partners in a streamlined way that adds value for them as well as delivering the national targets and strategies.

7.29 In future, the LSC will focus more on strategic commissioning, ensuring that there is in every area a diverse and dynamic range of high quality post-16 providers able to meet the needs of all learners. Working as a key part of the local authority led strategy for ensuring the delivery of the 14-19 entitlement in each local area, the LSC will fund colleges, sixth forms and training providers to play their part in delivering the entitlement. The LSC will remain responsible for the efficient and effective use of its budgets. It will have stronger powers of intervention to tackle failing and mediocre provision, taking on a number of powers transferred from the Secretary of State. It will develop its funding methods so that they are increasingly driven by the choices of learners and employers, making a decisive shift to a demand-led approach.

7.30 Working with partners locally, regionally and nationally, the LSC will integrate training and skills with other services so that they have maximum impact on employment, economic regeneration and social inclusion. Its relationship with colleges and training providers will be more strategic and more selective, with less operational involvement, with a strong commitment to avoiding bureaucracy, thereby creating space for the good to flourish combined with a powerful focus on tackling underperformance.

7.31 As explained in Chapter 4, work is in hand to simplify quality assurance and improvement through the establishment of the QIA and the creation of a single inspectorate. The roles and responsibilities are:

Department for Education and Skills	Sets overall policy framework for sector. No operational role in quality improvement. Operational work of DfES Standards and Skills for Life Units transfers to partners.
Learning and Skills Council	Applies evidence and data on quality to inform planning and funding decisions. No operational involvement in inspection or quality improvement services.
Quality Improvement Agency	Formed from part of the Learning and Skills Development Agency. Leads development and implementation of single, integrated quality improvement strategy for FE sector. Commissions services to support quality improvement action by colleges and providers.
Ofsted and Adult Learning Inspectorate	New single inspectorate from April 2007 will provide inspection services. No operational role in working with individual institutions to improve quality.
Centre for Excellence in Leadership	Provides programme of leadership and management development training and sector leadership strategies. Integrated within QIS.
Lifelong Learning UK	The SSC which defines skills standards needed for staff working in post-16 education and training, as basis for design of staff training programmes. Integrated within QIS. Manages the collection, and interpretation, of staff data.

7.32 Our major reform programme, particularly the introduction of the new 14-19 entitlement, will require much closer working between the school and college workforces and organisations that support them. The Centre for Excellence will need to work closely with the National College of School Leadership and the Leadership Foundation for Higher Education. Looking ahead, we will consider whether there is scope and need for closer integration. LLUK will need to strengthen joint working with the Training and Development Agency for Schools (TDA) and the Skills for Care and Development Sector Skills Council.

We are clarifying roles in the regions

7.33 As a result of the LSC's new business cycle, most providers will now have a 'single conversation' with the LSC covering local, regional and sectoral needs. The LSC will build on the initial experience of incorporating SSAs into the annual business cycle to inform planning and purchasing, working towards a position where robust SSC intelligence drives all relevant provision and is reflected in regional, local and provider plans.

7.34 As part of its restructuring, the LSC is strengthening its capacity to plan and commission with partners the skills infrastructure needed across the region to meet the needs of employers and adults, and to oversee competitions for new provision. That will be backed up by a stronger non-executive regional structure. At local level, the LSC is establishing 148 LSC partnership teams, covering the same areas as local authorities, so that it can work directly with those authorities and children's trusts. This will support the 14-19 reforms in particular.

7.35 The strengthened regional and local tiers and stronger links between jobs, training and skills in cities, means that the current structure of 47 local LSCs will need to change. We will ask the Chair of the LSC to advise on a new streamlined accountability structure, which secures strong engagement of employers and other stakeholders.

7.36 We agree with Sir Andrew Foster's proposition that we should establish a review of activity at regional level to ensure mechanisms at this level are coordinated and coherent. We will pursue with regional partners how best to achieve this including identifying an appropriate external organisation to conduct the review.

7.37 We will continue to strengthen the links both at regional and at city level between activities to improve jobs, skills, and economic development. We will also continue to bring together support for jobs and skills, as set out in Budget 2006. (See case study opposite). Skills feature increasingly strongly as a key driver of regional productivity and growth in the Regional Economic Strategies. From April 2007 there will be Local Area Agreements everywhere between the Government and local authorities and their partners. The LSC will work with local authorities to ensure that the skills provision supports the local priorities reflected in these agreements. In the major cities, last autumn's 'city summits', now followed by the recent State of the Cities report, highlighted the need for action on employment and skills to be better aligned – particularly to help tackle concentrations of worklessness in the big cities.

7.38 The big cities are now preparing to respond to Government with their proposals. There is a lot of interest in developing city-wide (or city region-wide) approaches – for instance building on the 'city skills boards' already set up in Manchester and Nottingham to steer the work of the key agencies so that the skills provision reflects the needs of local people and employers. The recent Welfare Reform Green Paper proposed trials of local consortia to provide a focus for co-ordinating cross-agency efforts to reduce the high numbers of jobless people in cities. The change in the structure of local LSCs will help ensure that, together with Jobcentre Plus, the RDA, and the local authorities, and employers, better integrated, flexible and locally responsive strategies are developed for each area.

Jobs and Skills

In July 2005, the Matthew Boulton College of Further and Higher Education in Birmingham relocated to new state-of-the-art premises in the city's Eastside Learning Zone. The college worked with its partners to develop effective support services and training for business and individuals including an on site Jobcentre Plus presence.

The Jobcentre Plus, Connexions and the college's other advice and guidance services are integrated to provide comprehensive and coherent support to people seeking to train, retrain or up-skill. Lone parents, people on working-age benefits, new migrants and older workers in particular are benefiting from the service. There are also advantages for employers as the centre staff can use their up-to date local labour market knowledge to make links between business priorities, training and jobs, helping to supply Birmingham with well-equipped job-ready people.

The presence of Jobcentre Plus on site facilitates a skills exchange between employment experts and college staff which enriches their practice. It also brings in employers, who make a wider contribution to the effectiveness of the college.

Colleges and other providers define their own mission and should work with others where that would raise standards or broaden opportunity

7.39 In reshaping and clarifying the roles of all those who work with colleges, we seek to reinforce the role of the autonomous, independent college. A college, led by its governing body, is responsible for determining its own mission, managing its own affairs, meeting its statutory responsibilities and improving its own performance. Each governing body needs to identify and regularly review the mission which will best enable it to meet the needs of its local community, including employers, and contribute to national economic and social priorities. We want each governing body to play a stronger and more active role in defining the college's distinctive excellence, and take a more robust approach to ending activities which are not being done well, or are not core to the mission.

7.40 Each college is also part of a wider system. The 14-19 reforms in particular require strong partnerships – and we look to all colleges to play the role that will best contribute to the local entitlement and provide young people with the best opportunities to achieve and succeed. Each college therefore also needs to assess the contribution it can make towards the wider purpose. And we want each governing body to keep under review options for collaboration, federation and merger.

7.41 Overall, the proposals in this White Paper will strengthen the role and profile of governing bodies in leading their colleges. Our plans for increasing self-regulation will be important in defining the role and responsibilities of governing bodies. We are confident that the great majority will rise to the challenge, building on the powerful contribution they already make, and we will ensure they are supported to do so.

7.42 We will shortly be publishing revised model Instruments and Articles which will implement the changes proposed in the 2004 governance consultation. We also need to ensure that we have a governance framework which meets our future needs and supports greater autonomy, initiative and responsiveness. So, we will draw up, in consultation, a revised governance framework which will aim to facilitate increased diversity and build on best governance practice. We will continue work with the LSC, the CEL, the AoC and colleges to develop a Good Governance Guide to spread best practice, and other materials to help promote the role and opportunities more widely, to an appropriate and diverse audience. This will be backed up by governor training and development, and support for recruitment campaigns. We will encourage employers to allow staff time to participate in college governance as part of their commitment to community activity.

7.43 Other providers in the learning and skills sector are also responsible for determining their own mission, and managing their own affairs including improving performance. Their responsibilities will vary according to the nature of the provider. For example many independent providers focus on specific work based learning, and voluntary and community-based providers often focus on stepping stone provision or PCDL. But it will also be vital that they assess, within the context of their specific remit, the contribution they can make to the local area through greater collaboration.

There will be a new national learning model

7.44 In order to inform the workings of the system as a whole, we will develop a new 'national learning model' as recommended by Sir Andrew Foster. The model will bring together the analysis of skills needs from the demand side with trends in provision of learning, in order to drive decisions on priorities and funding allocations.

7.45 Many of the component parts already exist. The Leitch review has developed a model for projecting long term skills needs for the economy. There is extensive data on sectoral and regional skills gaps and priorities assembled by the Skills for Business network and Regional Skills Partnerships, and the LSC's National Employer Skills Survey. There are national datasets on achievement of qualifications and patterns of training activity, and progression from the schools system and into HE. There is data on demography and migration as they affect both supply and demand for skills. We have clear Public Service Agreement targets for skills and qualifications set in successive spending reviews. The LSC's annual business cycle already determines the planning framework for the allocation of public funds on the basis of much of this information. SSAs commit public and employer funds to purposes agreed with employers.

7.46 We will work with the Skills Alliance to draw these elements together into a nationally agreed and published learning and skills assessment setting out the skills priorities for the future, the implications for targets, and the funding principles that underpin them. It will be produced on a rolling three year basis, with the first published in 2007 linked to the outcome of the Comprehensive Spending Review.

Chapter 8: Impact and outcomes

Clarity about the shared outcome we are all seeking will help everyone understand the role they play and the contribution they make to the overall mission. There is a set of outcomes we should be aiming to secure collectively for learners, for employers and for providers.

We have developed a draft outcomes framework to summarise these, and would welcome views on this.

8.1 The proposals in this White Paper set out a way forward to prepare the FE system to meet future challenges. The central goal is providing the skills we need for an economy that will sustain our quality of life and our international standing. Successful reform of such a large and complex public service requires us to be clear about the impact we are seeking to secure for different stakeholders, and how the various strands of reform contribute to achieving that impact.

Impact on learners

8.2 Although learners vary enormously in their needs and motivations, and study in very different settings, there is a set of outcomes we should aim to secure for all.

Through these reforms we seek the following outcomes for learners:

- Learner success is the top priority: the system focuses on giving learners the preparation they need to achieve their ambitions and progress in life and at work.
- Learning programmes are tailored to each individual's needs and aspirations. 14-19 year-olds are supported and encouraged to choose the combination of programmes best able to prepare them for success in life; adults to get the skills they need for employment and progression.
- Learners receive good advice and guidance. It helps them to choose the programme and institution best meeting their needs, overcome stereotyping, and make good choices about progression to employment or further learning.
- Learners are valued and respected as customers, and their views and requirements are used to shape provision.
- Learners are taught by staff who are expert, highly motivated, well-trained professionals, working in attractive, well-equipped premises.
- The qualifications system enables learners to gain recognition for their achievements and show employers what they have learnt and so supports their employment prospects.
- Learners are provided with fair access to learning opportunities. Barriers to learning faced by some groups are tackled by effective systems to ensure equality of treatment and availability of support.

Impact on employers

8.3 The needs of employers and learners are not always identical. If we are to meet the long-term skills needs of the economy anticipated in Lord Leitch's Interim Report, we need employers to become much more demanding of skills and training. We will build on what has already been achieved through the Skills Strategy in making FE much more responsive to employers' needs.

Through these reforms, we seek the following outcomes for employers:

- Employers benefit from providers whose core mission is to prepare their students well for successful employment in a modern economy.
- Employers are valued and respected as customers, and their views and requirements are used to shape provision.
- The Train to Gain programme gives employers power over the design and delivery of workplace training. The training can range from basic skills through to HE, sourced as a single package.
- Employers benefit from greater choice as new providers enter the market.
- Learning programmes are delivered by staff who have a good, up-to-date understanding of the world of work, with new opportunities for exchange of staff and expertise between employers and providers.
- The qualifications system makes it easy for employers to understand what each qualification represents in terms of level, breadth and skills gained. Through SSC-led Sector Qualifications Strategies, employers will determine the skills outcomes that qualifications should deliver.

Impact on providers

8.4 These ambitions for learners and employers can only be met through the work of schools, colleges and other providers. The public response to the Foster report, and the consultations that have informed this White Paper, have indicated a widespread recognition of the need for reform. We need to build on this to secure the enthusiastic participation of providers wanting to make these reforms work, with effective support from national agencies, and the removal of unnecessary barriers.

Through these reforms, we seek the following impact for providers:

- Providers benefit from increased understanding and esteem, on the part of the public and employers, for the contribution that the FE system makes to the economy and the nation.
- Providers are clear about what is expected, and there is consistency between the definition of mission and purpose, the use of performance indicators and success measures, and the setting of funding priorities.
- The planning and funding system is fair, straightforward to administer, and transparent. It operates with a proportionate touch, avoiding bureaucracy, unnecessary intervention and micro-management.
- There are rewards, including capital investment and lighter-touch inspection, for those who successfully meet the needs of learners and employers, and opportunities for the enterprising to expand.
- Providers are respected for their professionalism, with trust in good providers to do what is right for learners and employers, reflected in increased self-regulation and a commitment to self-improvement.
- Providers have the tools they need to do the job successfully: good teaching, learning and assessment materials, and a qualifications framework that is fit for purpose. Providers have the coherent and effective support they want for their own drive for quality improvement.
- Providers enjoy greater autonomy and a more streamlined system. This will simplify and reduce the burden of interventions, data requests, inspections and planning and funding mechanisms.

Outcomes framework

8.5 The *Every Child Matters* outcomes framework has demonstrated the power of a unified framework which creates a shared understanding amongst all the elements of a complex service about what each is contributing to the larger purpose. That framework was developed through an extensive process of consultation, and is now widely used in schools and children's services as a common reference point.

8.6 We would like to develop a comparable framework for post-16 education, training and skills. It starts, of course, from the *Every Child Matters* outcomes for young people up to the age of 19 and goes on to express the skills, qualifications and employment outcomes we are seeking for adults and employers as well.

8.7 A draft framework is shown in the attached chart. It reflects previous consultations on the 14-19 and skills strategies. For each group, the framework shows the high level aims, how they relate to key targets and indicators, and the benefits sought. We will consult on the substance of the framework and how it could be developed and used. We will discuss with Ofsted and the Adult Learning Inspectorate how it can inform the Common Inspection Framework used to inspect colleges and training providers.

Building reputation

8.8 Sir Andrew Foster's report noted that the FE system does not enjoy a high profile or a strong reputation compared with other parts of the education service.

8.9 We believe that the combination of a clear mission focused on economic impact, combined with resolute action to drive up quality, and a real focus on learner and employer needs, will do much to help the system improve its reputation. Sir Andrew Foster also advocated a review of reputation management to look at how the Government, the LSC, colleges and other providers could improve the way the system and its benefits are promoted. We agree and have commissioned a review to inform the development of proposals for a communication strategy.

8.10 Meanwhile, we welcome the steps that colleges and providers themselves are taking to strengthen their voice and raise their own profile nationally and locally, including through the AoC. It is right that colleges should take a lead in ensuring public understanding of what they do. We look to the major national representative organisations to take a stronger role in promoting the excellence and reputation of the sector and in facing up to weaknesses.

Celebrating success

8.11 An important part of building the reputation of the sector is celebrating its successes. We will continue to highlight the achievements of colleges and the wider learning and skills system in a number of ways. Learning and Skills Beacon status is awarded to providers demonstrating excellence in teaching and learning, supported by strong leadership and management. The STAR Awards recognise excellent individuals such as teachers, trainers, managers and support staff. The Apprenticeship Awards recognise employers who have demonstrated the business benefits of Apprenticeships and apprentices who have excelled in their learning.

8.12 The UK bid to host WorldSkills 2011 has the potential to boost significantly the reputation of the sector. In the run-up to 2011, whether or not the UK bid succeeds, we will look to find ways to re-energise the UK's framework for skills competitions to recognise the achievement of world class skills by individuals and drive skills improvements in different sectors. This work is being led by UK Skills supported by a UK-wide coalition of partners.

WorldSkills 2005

Andrew Blair from County Antrim won the Gold Medal in the Autobody Repair Competition at the 2005 WorldSkills Competition in Helsinki. The recognition he has received since then has changed public perceptions towards skills. He says: "Some people think that only people who did badly at school work in a garage. I hope my Gold Medal will show them they're wrong. It was great to represent my country and to beat off strong challenges from Japan and Korea proving that the UK is the world's best for autobody repair."

Andrew's training provider, Blackwater House, has been inundated with young people wanting to follow in his footsteps. Andrew gives induction presentations and acts as a mentor. Apprenticeship applications are up 25%, the drop-out rate has reduced almost to zero and achievement rates are 100%. Local young people are leaving school not only wanting to join the motor trade but bringing with them a much higher level of prior achievement, reversing traditional perceptions and boosting the reputation of the trade.

Andrew's employer agrees that his overall skill set is perfect for the job. As well as his technical expertise, he has good communication, organisational and problem solving skills. He works well with other employees, passing on the wider skills he has acquired through WorldSkills. This is a great asset for the business as it means employees are always learning and improving, providing better customer service and quality of work.

8.13 We will look to find ways to draw together the array of skills competitions into a single framework building up from local to international level, giving skills achievements a higher public profile. Linking colleges and their staff with the supply of winning competitors and expert trainers will associate the sector with excellence. The QIA, working with UK Skills and Investors in People, will undertake a parallel review of Beacon status, STAR awards, the National Training Awards, and other means of celebrating success, to consider how they can be integrated into the new framework for recognising world class achievement in skills by individuals and organisations.

8.14 If the UK bid for WorldSkills 2011 succeeds, we will have an unprecedented opportunity to mount a 5 year skills campaign, linked to the 2012 Olympics, and culminating in 2011 with a major celebration of world class skills provision and achievement in the UK.

Printed in the UK for The Stationery Office Limited
on behalf of the Controller of Her Majesty's Stationery Office
167682 3/06 JW4524